C000004761

Passing on the Love

A life spent in a caring profession

By Dee Roberts
With Diane Morrison

Dee Roberts

17 · 2 · 19

An environmentally friendly book printed and bound in
England by www.printondemand-worldwide.com

Mixed Sources
Product group from well-managed
forests, and other controlled sources
www.fsc.org Cert no. TT-COC-002641
© 1996 Forest Stewardship Council
FSC

PEFC
PEFC/16-33-415

PEFC Certified
This product is
from sustainably
managed forests
and controlled
sources
www.pefc.org

This book is made entirely of chain-of-custody materials

www.fast-print.net/store.php

PASSING ON THE LOVE

A catalogue record for this book is available from the
British Library

ISBN 978-178035-790-4

First published 2014 by
FASTPRINT PUBLISHING
Peterborough, England.

Thanks to the staff in the café of Woking
Garden Centre in Egley Road, who kept me fed
and watered over the many months of writing.
I can wholeheartedly recommend their special
over-sixties lunch
on Mondays and Tuesdays!

Thanks especially to the friends and family
who encouraged me
to put my stories onto paper.

Thanks also to Diane Morrison, for
interpreting my scribbling and making sense
of my ramblings; to Christine Grew, Chris
Hayhoe and Marjorie Kiddle who helped with
the proof-reading and to John Durrant for his
skilful enhancement of my photos.

Promotion to Sister 1968

Introduction

For several years many people have been urging me to gather all my experiences together into a book but I never really took their suggestions seriously. Then, in June 2013, I was on holiday in Northumberland with my cousin Sue and friend Pam, reminiscing with them about various things that had happened, when Sue told me, with some emphasis to get it written down! She followed this up every time we spoke on the phone thereafter, encouraging me to keep at it, and once I had started I was amazed at how much came back to me.

I have never kept a diary so this account is written solely from memory, with a little help from two Diagnosis Books and a Delivery Case Book from my training days. We all recall things differently, and our recollections differ depending on the position from which we viewed the event. If you were present on any of the occasions I describe and remember them differently, I have been truthful as far as is humanly possible and no offence is meant to anyone. If you were working elsewhere as a midwife or a nurse in the sixties, seventies and eighties I hope my anecdotes will bring to mind memories of your own.

Many of the stories are amusing but it is important to stress that they all occurred amidst much hard work – the daily grind that is life most of the time, but would make very dry reading if detailed in full! Also, I have met and worked with many dedicated and caring people over the years, all of them with their own unique story to tell that would make at least as good a read as mine. It is always a joy to meet up with former colleagues and I salute every one of them.

The second half of the twentieth century, in which I lived my working life, saw more major advances in medicine and science, and faster change in nursing practice and society in general than any previous era. Some of these have been very much for the better, some seem to have been for the worse, but babies will always be born and human beings will always have the same fundamental needs. I have been sustained through the highs and lows of my own life by the constant, unconditional love of God and the family and good friends He has provided. This is the tale of how I have humbly attempted to care for others as He has cared for me.

It all began in a small village on a small island, just as the world stood on the brink of momentous events...

Early Years

Chapter One

I made my entrance into the world one Sunday lunchtime in February 1941, and I made it fast. "This one will always be in a hurry!" the midwife at the Princes Mead Nursing Home predicted to my mother – but I went on to spend twenty-nine years in a profession where patience is not just a virtue, but a necessity.

The Isle of Wight was gearing up for war and, in its north-eastern corner where we lived, my father, Wilf, was involved with the Fire Service. He and my mother, Connie, had been married for eleven years and there had been only one previous pregnancy, a stillborn boy, severely abnormal, delivered also at high speed by my mother alone on the kitchen floor. Consequently she had been very anxious while carrying me and I was much wanted, loved and prayed for.

My earliest memories are of idyllic days spent on the beach and in the fields surrounding the village of Seaview – an only child, shy and rather lonely. One of my favourite beaches was the one beside Seaview Pier, a beautiful chain pier built in 1881 and designed by a local architect. More than a thousand feet long and fifteen feet wide it was suspended from four towers and used by the Navy during the war. Afterwards it fell into disrepair and was severely damaged by storms in the early fifties. The pier head – all that was left standing, was demolished in 1952.

Half a mile up the road lived my maternal grandmother, whom I remember as a little old lady with white hair, usually dressed in black with a white collar and always ready with a smile and a welcome. Her cottage was primitive even for those days, with an outside toilet, wash house and a black coal range. One day when I was about six years old I was sent there with some kippers my Mum had bought for her in Ryde, and made my way across the field carefully clutching the paper bag at the top. Meanwhile the bottom was becoming steadily soggier and at last it disintegrated, depositing the kippers right in the middle of a large, fresh cowpat!

I stood looking at them as they gradually sank into the foul mess and burst into tears. When I arrived at Gran's sobbing my heart out it took her a while to extract from me what had happened but, when she understood, she took my hand and said: "I'm sure it's not that bad; maybe we can rescue them!" She was ever the optimist but when we walked back to the scene of the catastrophe and saw the evidence even she had to accept that there would definitely be no kippers for tea that night!

Gran had grown up in Bristol in a George Muller Home (similar to Dr Barnardo's) and met my grandfather when they were both in service at Seagrove Manor in Seaview – she as a maid, he as a gardener. On their marriage they were given the lodge at the Manor gate to live in, and later moved up the hill to nearby Nettlestone. Grandad Wheeler died in 1946 when I was five, and Gran in 1957, just a few days after celebrating her 84th birthday with a party underneath the walnut tree in her garden.

My first experience of hospital was at the age of three when I had the glands in my abdomen removed because of TB. The Children's Ward was a glassed-in veranda and visiting was strictly limited; not surprisingly, I remember nothing first-hand about any of this. Three years later I went down with pneumonia and this time was nursed at home. I remember the cotton wool jacket I had to wear and having small pieces pulled off each day when I was improving. The following winter, as a preventative measure, I was made to wear the dreaded liberty bodice!

It was this experience (the illness, not the liberty bodice!) that first aroused my interest in nursing – I liked the idea of looking after people and making them better and, from then on I never wanted to be anything else but a nurse. My dolls and teddies were forever being nursed and 'made better' in my own pretend 'hospital'. Later on I devoured books about nursing; *Yes, Matron*, the memoir of Gladys Hardy, was given to me as a school prize; *Come Hither, Nurse* by Jane Grant, a light-hearted account of a nurse's three years of training, was another favourite, one I suspect might be published under a different title today!

Reading had not come easily to me. I attended Nettlestone Primary School, as my mother had done before me, but took a long time to achieve both literacy and numeracy. With extra tuition in the holidays from a friend of the family who was also a teacher I soon caught up and became a bookworm, devouring adventure stories. My favourites were anything by Enid Blyton, especially the *Malory Towers* series.

Summer holidays weren't all work and study; every year the Christian Seaside Mission came to our village and held children's holiday meetings for two or three weeks on the beach. Each morning a sand 'pulpit' was built and decorated with shells – often a verse from the Bible was picked out on the front with flowers. A lot of these flowers came from our garden and, as the days passed, it became somewhat devoid of colour! When I ran out of flowers of our own I would try to beg some from the wife of the GP who lived opposite or, if all else failed, pick anything that I found hanging over a wall!

In the mornings we listened to Bible stories and learned choruses; in the afternoons we had races, treasure hunts, tea parties and quizzes. Sometimes the leaders would walk around the village in disguise and we would play 'Hunt the Leader'. I loved all these activities and they formed the basis for the Christian faith which has underpinned my life.

At the age of ten, my parents decided that I should learn to play the piano. This was not one of their better ideas as I had no musical aptitude whatsoever and hated practicing in the cold front room where our piano lived. Every Saturday morning another local girl and I rode our bikes round the sea-wall to Ryde for a lesson at ten o'clock. We each had half an hour, the first would wait for the second and then we would ride home together. The teacher sat on my left-hand side knitting while I played, and every time I made a mistake she would tap my hand with her knitting needle. When she did this the knitting frequently came off the needles, and I was very prone to making mistakes so her knitting didn't grow much while I was having lessons!

Fortunately this project didn't last long, though I did enjoy the bike rides – I had a blue bike of which I was very proud and which I was allowed to ride to school as well. One lunchtime I was on my way home, needing to take the right fork in the road and, with a car behind me, needing to signal my intentions. As I quite often did, I indicated with my leg rather than my arm, though this did make the bike wobble rather more. When I got home I was in for a telling-off from my Dad – it had been him in the car behind me!

After taking my eleven-plus, I went to Ryde Secondary Modern School where I gained six GCEs. Around this time I started to spend a lot of time with my cousin, Sue; I am told that, although we argued a lot, if either one of us was in trouble we would immediately 'gang up' on the adults! It was good to have her company. After we left school she worked sometimes in the Isle of Wight Telephone Exchange, sometimes in the Cosham Exchange at Portsmouth, before moving to Leicestershire where she still lives.

Following the Hungarian Uprising in the autumn of 1956, two-hundred thousand or more people fled Hungary to escape Soviet reprisals. Many came to Britain and an old army camp on the outskirts of Seaview was designated as a refugee camp for them. We fifth-form pupils at my school were organised into teams to clean the huts and make up beds and bunks; the one I was allocated to clean had been used by officers during the war and was now going to house families. The huts had cleaned up very well and soon became home for the steady stream of displaced Hungarians that began to arrive in November – mostly young men from Budapest. This dramatically swelled the population of our little village and there was some concern expressed locally about all these men, uprooted from their homes and with nothing to do.

On the Sunday afternoon before Christmas I was at a carol service in Beulah Chapel with my Mum when a family who were obviously refugees came in –parents with three children, one just a baby. They had been attracted by the singing and the warmth – it was very cold outside – but did not stay long as they could speak no English. On the way home my Mum decided that we should invite them to Christmas dinner if Dad agreed. He had no problem at all with this plan, so we dashed back down the hill to look for them. By this time it was nearly dark but eventually we found them huddling in the doorway of the bakery and persuaded them to come back with us for a cup of tea and a warm up. Somehow the invitation was made and understood.

On Christmas day the family arrived on the doorstep as smartly dressed as they could manage. The man was embarrassed that he had not been able to shave, and very grateful when my Dad gave him a razor to use and then take back to the camp with him. Our home was quite small but we all managed to fit around the table once it was fully extended and there was plenty of food for everyone.

Their elderly grandmother had come with them and sat next to my gran, the two ladies smiling and patting each others' hands, friends without a word of language in common. In the afternoon we went to the front room which we only used at Christmas (or for my short-lived piano practice!). Dad and I had decorated it and there was the tree with lights twinkling merrily and gifts for everyone underneath, with toys and biscuits for the children. Our visitors sang *Silent Night* to us in Hungarian and then we all joined in singing together. It was one of the best childhood Christmases I ever had.

We saw quite a lot of the family during the three months they spent at the camp. When I visited them there, I found that they were occupying one of the rooms I had helped to clean. Around Easter they moved to London where the father of the family had been found a job as a pastry chef in a hotel. I often wonder what, if anything, those children remember of the time they spent on the Isle of Wight.

The pre-nursing course I began at the age of sixteen involved an hour's journey on two buses to Newport Grammar School, but I enjoyed the experience very much. There were a dozen students, most from secondary modern schools and two or three from the Grammar School where we were incorporated into the sixth form as an independent stream. We had one school year – September to July – studying anatomy and physiology, including two weeks hands-on experience at St Mary's Hospital in Newport, and ending with our first preliminary examination, Prelim I. (Prelim II was taken after the first year of general training.)

After Easter 1958 I had my first work experience at St Mary's, on the Medical Ward in the old workhouse buildings. For the first time I lived away from my parents in the Nurses Home and walked each day to the ward, which was at the bottom of the hill near a duck pond. The modern wards, Operating Theatre and Maternity Unit were at the top of the hill, as was the dining room – the time it took us to get there was part of our lunch hour, leaving less time to eat the actual meal. The workhouse wards had something of a stigma attached to them and the patients disliked being in them.

I remember on my first day, arriving to find the Sister very busy and being told to wander round the ward familiarising myself. The patients were resting after lunch with the curtains round their beds half pulled and, as I walked through several bays with up to six beds in each, I peered cautiously in at some of them. All were still and quiet but one man seemed unnaturally so. As soon as I saw him I said to myself, 'He's dead.'

Back at the office, Sister was on the phone and I waited quietly for her to finish, wishing she would hurry up, hoping I was wrong but, at the same time, hoping I was right. I was also wondering how to put it to her respectfully! In the end I said: "I've never seen a dead person before but I think that man in room three has died."

"Oh my dear," she said, "we'd better go and see!"

Together we walked back to room three, and she peered through the curtain just as I had. "Well," she conceded, "you seem to be right!" That was my baptism of fire!

The Sister was something of a character, as many were in those days. Faced by a loud braggart announcing himself as "Colonel Taylor, OBE!" she replied with her own name and title followed by "SRN, SCM, BO!" ...BO being medical code for 'Bowels Open'! The colonel was from Seaview and I felt terribly ashamed to come from the same village as such a pompous old man. But Sister was very kind, lending me her red-lined cape to walk up the long cinder path for coffee and lunch – I felt like a real nurse in that! First coffee breaks on Monday and Tuesdays were always popular because toast and dripping was served, but we had to finish our lunches quickly because we all had to stand up when Matron left the dining room.

The trained nurses looked after us well, showing us interesting things and explaining what was happening. There was still much talk about the Shalcombe Down air crash of November the previous year when a plane had come down in a chalk pit, killing forty-five people and injuring thirteen. Major incidents like this were few and far between on the Isle of Wight and green trainees made a good audience for ghoulish stories about 'the smell of pork cooking'! Flowers were permitted in hospitals in those days, but all the vases were taken out of the wards every night and not returned in the morning until the cleaning and dusting was completed. Each vase had clean water and the flowers redone daily but care had to be taken, as many Sisters were quite superstitious and it was considered a herald of death if red and white flowers were arranged together (blood and bandages!).

Much of the work during my two weeks on-the-job training involved the treating of pressure areas on heels, elbows and buttocks to prevent sores, and cleaning incontinent patients using 'tow', a cotton by-product. This in no way put me off and I started applying to different hospitals to do my general training. I had, until then, led a somewhat quiet life. After the war, my father came out of the Fire Service and ran a building firm in partnership with a friend for the rest of his working life. The company bought the land along the drive to Seagrove Manor, divided it into plots and built houses there in the mid-fifties. Halfway up the drive was our house, named Staddlestones because some of the mushroom-shaped staddlestones from the old drive had been kept and put in our garden. My parents moved into it in 1959 but, apart from that, very little seemed to be happening on the Isle of Wight. In the interests of independence and a livelier existence I applied to train at the Royal Masonic Hospital in Ravenscourt Park, Hammersmith, was granted an interview and accepted.

The Masonic Hospital was a very impressive
red-brick building that had won an
architecture award for the best new building of
1933: large statues of Hebe the Greek goddess
of youth, and Aesculapius, the Greek god of
medicine and healing flanked its entrance.
Beyond this lay a vast front hall and each
ward had a large curved balcony overlooking
beautiful gardens with a lily pond. The
Wakefield Wing was only two years old, with
three wards, a Physiotherapy Department,
Pathology Lab, Chapel and Nursing-School
accommodation for Staff Nurses and third-
year students. It was connected to the main
Nurses Home by a tunnel and to the rest of
the hospital by a bridge.

In the main hospital each Unit was made up
of four four-bedded wards and nine single
rooms. Room thirteen was always named room
Z because nobody wanted to be in room
thirteen, though everybody knew Room Z was
the thirteenth room! The wards were arranged
alphabetically – A and B Units on the ground
floor, C and D on the first floor etc. Floor Four
was for private patients – student nurses
didn't work there. Everything at the hospital
happened in alphabetical order, even at
compulsory prayers – only Roman Catholic
nurses excused – we lined up in strict
alphabetical order with a gap where the one

Catholic nurse would have been. Sister Tutor
would enter the room and, as her feet touched
the carpet, we would all in unison sink to our
knees! (This routine only continued while in
Pre-Training School.)

The shoe supplier came to fit us all with two
pairs of brown lace-ups; these were mandatory
and often needed patching to cover the holes
made from kicking bed wheels into position!
These were worn with honey-coloured 'Aristoc'
stockings the seams of which had to be
straight. In hot weather some dispensed with
the stockings and pencilled a 'seam' in with an
eyebrow pencil. We made up our caps from an
oblong of starched cotton that had to be folded
to sit on top of the head with 'angels' wings'
coming down each side (made 'large' they
enabled us to have two big rollers in our hair if
we needed to look smart in the evening). These
were pinned with gold safety pins and we
always kept one made up in our rooms in case
of accidents with the sluice. This was where
bedpans and urinals were emptied and, if we
kicked the wrong tap, high pressure could
cause the water to shoot up to the ceiling and
fall onto our heads. This necessitated a long
wet walk back to our rooms dripping all the
way.

Each new intake of the PTS was called a Set
and, as we arrived at the beginning of

January1960 we were Set 1 – 1960. One of the first things we had to do was have a Heaf Test for tuberculosis, which was a lot more common in those days, as universal vaccination did not begin until 1953, though this has since been discontinued. There were eighteen of us living and working together in close proximity and we soon became close friends. The two school rooms were in the basement – one arranged as a classroom with desks (where we sat in alphabetical order of course!), the other as a small ward where we practiced basic skills such as lifting, washing, feeding and bed-making. Bandaging was a complicated affair in those days, as Tubigrip had not yet been invented. The capeline head and stump bandage was very difficult and took a lot of practice; we also learned spica bandaging, applying a many-tailed bandage to an abdomen, and T bandaging for the perineum. On one occasion I remember a chair leg getting incorporated in the bandaging, leaving the 'patient' unable to move at all!

Diet was very important in the recovery and healing process so, although we didn't cook, we had lectures on nutrition. When we got onto the wards we would have to deliver afternoon tea to the patients so we needed to practice serving sandwiches and cakes from a tray with a spoon and fork.

Each week there were visits to places like waterworks and museums.

At first, we went to the ward half a day a week to observe – I remember watching the dressing of an old war wound the size of a fist on a man's buttock the first morning I was there! We began to practice the things we learnt in school, such as blanket baths and the boiling of urine tests in glass test tubes over a Bunsen burner. Many of the tubes got cracked in the process but, fortunately, we didn't have to pay for the ones we broke, unlike thermometers which cost students sixpence or a shilling per breakage, paid at Matron's office. Each morning before breakfast while in PTS, we had to record our own TPRs (temperature, pulse and respiration readings).

The hospital was a pleasant place to work, open and airy and widely spread. Units A, C and E were surgical, B, D and F medical – I enjoyed working on the Surgical Wards best. Day shifts were 7.30am to 5pm or a split duty (morning and evening but not afternoon) 2 till 4, nights 8pm to 8am, supposedly four nights one week and five the next, but sometimes nine on and five off and often muddled together with only one night off. On day duty we had one day off a week and, if lucky, we finished at 2pm prior to our day off and started at 1pm the day after. It was rare to get two consecutive days off. The Nurses Home was comfortable enough but very close to the District Line. Back home on the Isle of Wight I had been used to falling asleep to the sound of the sea – here it was the sound of the Tube!

Each month we collected our pay from the School of Nursing – again in strict alphabetical order and if we missed our slot we had to return when everyone else had received their pay the following day. It came in cash in an envelope and started at less than ten pounds – there was great excitement when our pay went over the ten-pound mark! We always had a meal out as soon as we got our money – usually in the Hammersmith Wimpy Bar outside the tube station. By the end of our second year we could afford to eat at the Egg and Bacon Grill in Piccadilly Circus, and by the end of the third, at 'Half Guinea in the Piggy' off the Strand. This was a self-service buffet and, for half a guinea, the customer could eat as much as they liked, going back for seconds. On the first floor was a more lavish restaurant called 'Guinea in the Piggy': the food was better quality than downstairs and the all-you-can-eat price was a guinea. We also visited the Ritz Cafe opposite the Commodore Cinema, where we had spam fritters. Many evenings were spent in the Commodore (inevitably christened the

'Commode' by the nurses). In the winter it was so cold in there that we took hot water bottles in duffel bags.

The transportation of patients to and from wards, Theatre, Physio etc was done by a team of porters. Stationed at the front door to the Nurses Home was one we called the 'Professor'. He had returned from the war with what was then still called 'shell shock' and his behaviour was erratic enough to frighten some of the nurses, especially if they met him alone in the dark underground tunnel coming off duty. On one occasion late in the afternoon we heard the melody *Down Among the Dead Men* being played on the harmonium in the mortuary and, although we never knew for sure, we all believed it was the Professor playing. Concern for the feelings of recently bereaved relatives resulted in a hitherto undreamed-of breech of decorum – Matron was seen almost running down the main corridor to stop him!

The head porter sat in the entrance hall and wore a very smart uniform, but when he did come out from behind the front desk, he walked with a strange, swaying gait and was nicknamed the 'Camel'. Every morning at 10.45am the front hall was closed and the Camel would escort Matron, or the Senior Nurse on duty, to the small dais upon which rested the glass cabinet containing the Memorial Book. He would pull the drawer out, Matron would turn the page, he would close the drawer and then they would return in solemn procession to Matron's office. This ritual was sacrosanct and unvarying and extremely annoying for anyone sent to collect notes from the Administration Office that lay off the front hall. They were obliged to stand and twiddle their thumbs until the hall was reopened.

In some ways that first year seemed to last forever and in others it went by in a flash. I did six weeks in PTS, three months on a male Surgical Ward, six weeks back in school and then had two weeks holiday. The year ended with three months on a Medical Ward followed by night duty.

Chapter Two

For the first six months of our training we wore thick white cotton dresses like overalls. These made it very obvious to everyone that we were new and green as grass! When the six months were up we progressed to pale blue dresses with a white belt in the second year and a blue belt in the third year. The stiffly-starched white collars were held in place by studs at the front and back and were none-too comfortable.

We used small notebooks to record the details of the care we had given our patients during the past week, including all surgery and medication. These were called our Diagnosis Books and had to be completed and handed into the School of Nursing on a Sunday night for our tutor to mark. Alongside these we kept a Medicine Book, in which we recorded all the drugs we had used (in alphabetical order!) with a brief description of their use; by the end of training we should have used and understood the application of a wide variety of drugs.

At the commencement of training we were all issued with a printed Progress Experience book. It was our responsibility to ensure we kept it up to date and we had to get the Sister to sign it for the procedures we had witnessed and performed. Any extra-special experience was recorded by the Sister at the end of the book. It had to be completed for each Unit and when we moved onto the next Unit it had to be submitted to the School of Nursing so that our tutors could check our progress.

Working on the Surgical Wards it was important that we became proficient in the successful sterilisation of equipment. This was done in large stainless steel cauldrons of boiling water and would nowadays be considered a 'health and safety nightmare'! Removing small kidney dishes with forceps was one thing, but doing the same with the large Winchester bottles was quite another. A sterile trolley needed to be prepared for the removal of clips and sutures or for replacing a dressing. This required planning and close co-operation with colleagues in order to keep the sterilisers in use and avoid de-sterilising someone else's instruments that were nearly ready to come out.

Modern inventions and developments have since made life much easier for both nurses and patients. With no intravenous monitors and pumps, drips and infusions involved somebody taking the time to count drops-per-minute and ensure they ran at the correct speed. Soon we were doing this in our sleep! There were two jobs, however, that I did not like at all. The first was were cleaning slimy false teeth and getting them back in – it was easy for bottom teeth to slip and the patient to be in danger of swallowing them. The second was emptying sputum mugs – the sight and the sound as the contents fell into the sluice was so disgusting that I decided I could never marry a man called Fleming, as every time I said the name I would heave!

Ward Sisters were, to a woman, terrifying. There was one whose mood we anxiously judged by how she held her bucket bag as she walked into the ward – if she swung it in a nonchalant manner all was well; if it was rigid, watch out! One day on the Medical Ward a colleague who wasn't very tall was having trouble getting some clothing out of a patient's wardrobe, so she stepped up into the cupboard to gain a few inches. Just then the Assistant Matron walked in on her rounds accompanied by Sister. Anything was preferable to having to explain what was going on to these two formidable women, so I managed to shut the wardrobe door and stand in front of it while they chatted to all four patients, none of whom gave us away! When the coast was at last clear, I let her out.

It was on this same ward that I had a problem with the tea and sugar tins – or rather their contents. One of the Charge

Nurse's responsibilities was to oversee the store cupboards and, as a junior, I had been delegated the simple task of putting those stores away. I emptied the packets of sugar into the tin with no trouble but somehow, when I did the same with the tea, a few tea leaves fell into the sugar and the more I tried to fish them out the further in they went. This awful misdemeanour, though not quite punishable by death, resulted in a major rebuke from the Charge Nurse, who could be even more intimidating than the Sister.

A Cleaning Book appeared every weekend with a list of chores to be performed and signed for. The more menial jobs went to the students, while the medicine cupboard and DDA cupboard (containing drugs covered by the Dangerous Drugs Act) were cleaned by trained nurses. This was long before the days of 'super bugs' but staphylococcus aureus and streptoccus had to be avoided, and cleanliness was definitely next to Godliness when it came to controlling cross-infection.

Twice a day we gathered around Sister's desk for report – in the morning this was to hear how the patients had passed the night and to be given instructions for the morning's work. We then had to report back on this at Second Report, which occurred between First Lunch and Second Lunch. Discipline and seniority ran hand in hand and we gathered in three groups depending on which rooms we looked after. The reports were always about teaching, with student nurses questioned by Sister and required to speak up to ensure that we understood what we were talking about.

During one lunchtime report the patient in the room opposite the office rang his bell. I went to answer it straight away but neglected to close the door so what followed was enjoyed by all those gathered in the office. The gentleman was very confused and had rung for help because he was having difficulties driving his car at the traffic lights! I told him I would help him but he was deaf and couldn't hear me, so I raised my voice several decibels and said loudly: "The traffic lights are changing; they are green!" I then made car engine revving noises. "We are round the corner – can you manage now?" I left him sitting holding an imaginary steering wheel and returned to the office where everyone was laughing. They complimented me on my sound effects, which they said were most impressive!

Great care was taken to ensure that our patients always had water to drink. The jugs were collected early in the morning by a Ward Orderly to be washed and were replaced by the students, each with a glass three-quarters filled and placed on the bedside locker in a position that the patient could easily reach, with the handle facing the patient, to the right or to the left according to preference. Some patients needed to have the water 'fed' to them in white china cups with spouts; this was not easy and often resulted in wet pyjamas.

The serving of lunch was conducted like a full military manoeuvre! Sister and the orderly presided over the heated food trolley in the kitchen, dishing up the food requested by each patient. The junior nurses ran to and fro with covered meals, sometimes having to stay to cut it up and feed to people. On one Unit, if we were slow getting back to the kitchen the Sister would proclaim loudly: "Where *are* the nurses? How can I serve meals without the nurses?" When there was no one available to give her hot plates from the oven, she would declare: "It's *hell* trying to serve meals without hot plates!" These mantras could be regularly heard on most days.

On another Unit, every lunchtime the Sister would look at the menu to see what was on offer and ask the orderly: "What day is it?" The orderly would always reply "It's Monday (for instance) – all day until twelve midnight!" If it was steak and kidney pie for lunch she would invariably comment: "It's Kate and Sidney!" After lunch we collected the dirty dishes so that we knew how much each patient had eaten. Feeding very ill patients was a job I enjoyed because it offered opportunities to get to know them – I hated to see nurses hurrying the food and just stuffing it into people.

One afternoon I returned to the ward from a rather mundane 2-4pm break spent just pottering around the Nurses Home. My colleague had been off at the same time and I asked her if she'd had a good time. "Oh yes," she said. "I've been over to Number Ten to have tea with the PM!" Sir Harold Macmillan, the prime Minister at the time, was her Godfather – this was the year before he was obliged to resign following the Profumo affair.

Our dental care was all provided by the hospital in-house. One morning during my second year I had to have a filling with local anaesthetic and then go on duty at 2pm. By mid afternoon my face was covered in a blotchy rash, which I put down as a reaction to the injection, until I passed Assistant Matron on my way to the dining room for tea at 4. She stopped me, asked about the rash and told me it had nothing to do with the dentist. "I think you have German measles!" she said, and sent me to my room with no tea. Shortly afterwards I found myself in an ambulance being transferred to the Western Fever Hospital in Fulham.

We had visited this place as students in PTS to see the Artificial Respiration Unit with its iron lungs – it had once treated all of West London for smallpox, diphtheria, typhus and scarlet fever. A long central passageway with a roof but open on both sides had around twelve pavilions of single cubicles leading off it. All the walls were white tiled from the floor to half way up and then glass from there to the ceiling; there was no privacy and no visitors were allowed. It was a miserable experience and I was very glad when, five interminable days later, I was able to return to the Nurses Home. The Western Fever Hospital was closed in 1979 and demolished to make way for houses and a park.

Towards the end of my second year of training I took on the responsibility of leading the local branch of the Student Nurses' Association. It was in this capacity that I was called to see Matron and duly presented myself with the toes of my shoes just touching the blue carpet in her office, wondering why I had been summoned. It turned out that other London hospitals, such as the Westminster and University College Hospital had their own silver belt buckles for the nurses; Matron thought that we should have one too so we held a competition, within the SNA, to design one for the Royal Masonic. It turned out to be quite a lengthy process. Some were designed by individuals, some by groups and a closing date was set for entries. Then all the designs were displayed so that the student nurses could vote for their favourites. The most popular were sent to a London silversmith and adjusted so that they could be made in silver – solid and not filigree – two came back for our consideration and a final decision was made.

Eventually I was called back to Matron's office to see the first consignment of the buckles. They looked very impressive and felt heavy and substantial in the hand. I had the honour of buying the very first one to be worn when I became a Staff Nurse. This did not happen until July 1963 – later for me than for my friends, as my Finals were delayed due to a back injury (more about this later).

During the second and third years of training we returned to the School of Nursing for a block of theory instruction, where lectures from Consultants were accompanied by practical demonstrations. We looked forward to this time in school because we had weekends off duty; I could get back to the Isle of Wight on a Friday evening and return to London on Sunday Night. One winter afternoon during a particularly bad storm the boat attempted to tie up at Portsmouth Hard. The first rope thrown from the boat, fastened and tightened, snapped because of the swell. When they tried to throw a rope from the harbour to the boat, the same thing happened. As two ropes were needed, fore and aft, to make it fast, the boat had to toss and roll all the way back to Ryde to get another.

The following weekend there was another gale and Dad accompanied me to Portsmouth Harbour. He looked amazed when, as soon as we were on the boat, I slipped off my fashionable knee-high boots and he asked me what on earth I was doing. Quite seriously I told him that if the boat sank the boots would fill with water and weigh me down! I had remembered the stories of an old fisherman uncle who said that he always removed his thigh-waders when returning from a fishing expedition if the sea became rough.

In those days it was acceptable for nurses to receive a small gift from a patient as long as it was not money. Chocolates and fruit were often left for the whole ward staff to enjoy, and just before Christmas there would sometimes be bottles of wine or spirits. One patient who came in and out quite regularly was a director of Marks and Spencer. He would leave stockings, sweaters and other items of clothing, having tactfully made enquiries during his treatment as to sizes and preferences.

Another lady I cared for after major surgery was married to a London florist and lived in Knightsbridge. During one visiting time soon before her discharge from the hospital, her husband asked if they could take another student nurse and myself out to dinner. This idea appealed very much and when the patient had recovered we received a written invitation to go to the Dorchester Hotel in Park Lane with them. Neither of us had ever been anywhere so grand! We accepted with alacrity and then quickly realised we had 'nothing to wear'. I remember going to the West End and finding the perfect 'little black dress' (short, but not *too* short!) made of velvet with a small rosette flower at the neckline.

A couple of days before our evening out, there was a telephone message asking us if we would mind going to the Savoy instead of the Dorchester – as if we'd know the difference! The Dorchester, it seemed, did not have a floor show on the chosen night. Time off duty was requested and granted so that we could go to Mr Teasy-Weasy's hairdressers in the afternoon. Then, having made sure we had late passes until 11.30pm, we were collected by a chauffeur in an amazing limousine. He drove us to a mansion block of apartments, parked the car, and took us up several floors to our former patient's amazing home. My first impression was of the massive flower arrangement in the entrance hall and how the scent of it filled the air.

Following drinks and nibbles the driver took us to the Savoy and we followed our hosts into the dining room, hoping our little black dresses would pass muster. We were shown to a table next to the dance floor, where our first course was oysters – I was not greatly impressed with those and have never had them since – but the rest of the meal was fantastic, especially the pudding, a rich concoction of fresh fruit, meringue, cream, liqueur and sponge. A bit different to spam fritters at the Ritz Café!

In between each course our host danced with each of us whenever the orchestra played a gentle waltz. Having three ladies to accommodate he was kept very busy and the meal was a lengthy business. Cinderella-like we just made it back to the Nurses Home by 11.30 where it was back down to earth with the Professor at his desk waiting to check us in!

*

During our third year of training we were given more responsibility, which began by our being left 'in charge' while Sister went to a meeting, or for her supper break. On the first occasion this happened to me I was on a female General Surgical Ward. All was quiet, as it was evening visiting time and the lights were on low in the main corridor. Then out of the gloom, a phantom-like figure in full evening dress appeared round the corner. I must have looked startled because he said: "What's the matter, girl? Did you think I was the bloody undertaker?" Then I realised it was one of the gynaecologists coming to visit a patient!

I always preferred to be working on a Surgical Ward. Surgery in the sixties was not the relatively routine thing it is now, anaesthetics left people very nauseous and requiring antiemetic drugs. We often told people embarrassed by post-surgery wind *'it's better to belch and have the shame than to suffer the wind and have the pain!'* I nursed people recovering from gastectomy (for ulcers), abdominal-perineal resection of the rectum and lobectomy (both for cancer) and hiatus herniorrhaphy (another massive chest operation). When our patients improved enough they were transferred to a convalescent home.

Just before taking my final written exam (the State Finals) I was working on a male Surgical Ward and caring for a man who'd had a cancer

removed from his throat. He was very sick –
he'd had a tracheotomy and was fed through a
nasal-gastric tube: daily the fistula in his
throat was getting bigger and required
frequent cleaning. He was affectionately
known as Spu, and one thing he could still
enjoy was a Guinness at lunch time, which I
poured into his stomach via the tube with a
20ml syringe. I would never have made a
barmaid as I often got too much of a head on it
and made him burp! This went on for several
weeks with him shaking his fist at me every
time it happened and smiling broadly.

The State Finals consisted of a morning and
an afternoon paper. In between I visited the
ward to find out when I was off-duty the
following week. As I walked into the office the
Sister jumped up, pushed past me and
hurried away down the corridor. A few
minutes later she was back, asking me how
the morning paper had gone, and I then
returned to the examination room for the two-
and-a-half-hour surgical paper.

The next day I found out that Sister had
rushed out of the office to stop the porters
coming past wheeling the gurney that was
taking Spu to the mortuary – he had died
while I was sitting the morning paper. Sister
had known I would be upset and not wanted it

to affect my performance in the afternoon as I sat that important exam.

We did get fond of some of our really sick patients, but I always preferred to be on duty if they died so that I could perform the last offices for them – it seemed to complete the care. This was always a solemn occasion and done with all due respect. There were special sheets with a purple cross embroidered on them, and the body was wrapped into the sheet so that the purple cross was over the centre of the chest. The sheet was then sewn up. All the person's belongings had to be listed and packed up ready to be returned to the family.

On one happier occasion I was changing the top sheet following the blanket bath of an elderly gentleman. As we turned the top of it neatly back, a purple cross appeared. That sheet was removed very rapidly, discarded and replaced before he saw it! His time had not yet come.

*

Much was always made of Christmas at the hospital. Plans for the decorations started very early on some wards, as there was a competition for the best-decorated one and some Sisters threw themselves into it with gusto. A lot depended on the artistic abilities of the nurses allotted to the ward, and the themes were not necessarily religious – the one I remember best was 'India'. The Charge Nurse was a good artist and she drew friezes for the less gifted to colour in. Posters were obtained from local travel agents and all the staff wore Indian bangles and necklaces. When we were not working we had Indian scarves wrapped around us and each nurse was given a wooden elephant by Sister.

Every year during the run-up to Christmas there was a pantomime performed on a stage set up at the back of the dining room. The staff much enjoyed this home-grown entertainment, which included many 'in-jokes' and songs made up about hospital life and characters sung to the pop tunes of the day.

On the evening of Christmas Eve after we came off duty we would congregate in the Front Hall in uniform and wearing our short blue capes. We all lined up in Set order holding swaying lanterns in one hand and carol sheets in the other and Matron and Assistant Matron headed the procession as we went round the whole hospital singing carols. It was a long procession down dimly-lit corridors. Continuity was often lost and, if you were in the middle, you were often unsure whether to sing along with those in front or those behind! I have never understood why, but *Away in a Manger* was always sung on the Gynae Ward, which seemed rather unkind to those ladies who had just had hysterectomies.

At eleven o'clock we would make our way to the nearest church for Midnight Mass. On my last Christmas in London, after the service, we went back to a friend's flat and ended up with six of us sharing two double beds! No one slept much and we had to hurry in the morning to get back to the Nurses Home, put on our uniforms and be on duty by 7.30. Everyone worked all day Christmas Day and Boxing Day. There was no debate about it and no one could say it was unfair. During the day we were allowed to visit friends on other wards, view their decorations and have a 'drink' with them. Every year there was a Christmas meal put on for us – a big evening affair in the dining room.

After Christmas 1962 I went home for a week, taking with me a friend who had three nights off. It was the beginning of the notorious winter when we had nearly three months of snow and, most unusually for the Isle of Wight, our village was cut off due to the steep hills around it. My friend could not get back for duty, so we found the old sledge that the carpenter in my Dad's firm had made for me when I was a child. It had been stored in a shed and once the cobwebs and wildlife had been removed we had wonderful fun with it, joining the other folk out on the slopes – just so long as we managed to avoid the old bath in the middle of the field that was used as a water trough for the cows and horses.

Chapter Three

Our first night duty did not occur until the end of our first year of training. We were never left in charge at this stage, but during our second and third years we gradually assumed more responsibility. If there was no fully-trained nurse on the ward, Night Sister did her rounds between two and three in the morning and we all trooped down the corridors behind her, stopping outside all thirteen rooms, detailing the name, age and diagnoses of the patients, together with their treatment, surgery or drugs. In quiet times we would write letters, sew or read. Soon after *Lady Chatterley's Lover* was published in 1960, word went round that a colleague was reading it, concealed inside the dust-cover of a *Winnie the Pooh* book! How public opinion about what is 'acceptable' has changed in the last half-century...

Sometimes – unofficially – we would play cards. Once during Sister's round some playing cards slipped out of a colleague's uniform bib and fell to the floor one at a time. We had to walk back up that stretch of corridor and Sister very deliberately stepped over them without a word. At the end of her round she wished us goodnight with a broad and knowing smile!

Not all Sisters were so accommodating; some expected the night nurses to clear, clean and polish their desk tops every night – no matter if the ward was frantic, this ritual was sacrosanct and time had to be made for it. One particular desk I remember was as highly polished as a dance floor. We certainly had enough else to do. During the night the dressing drums had to be packed with cotton-wool swabs, gauze and 'bunnies' (sanitary towels) ready to go for sterilisation in the morning. On the Ear, Nose and Throat Ward nasal bolsters – tiny pillow-like pads with tape ties stitched on – had to be made for use when noses were bleeding or discharging. On the Eye Ward our somewhat alarming instructions for those recovering from cataract surgery was to *'pad and shackle'* for three nights to stop them knocking their eyes while asleep. The pad was placed over the eye and held firm with bandages and then the patient's wrists were tied to the cot sides leaving them unable even to scratch their nose should it itch!

Following more invasive surgery, some patients would have intravenous fluids given and a Ryles tube inserted via the nose into the stomach so that oral fluids could be gradually introduced. The nursing order in this situation would be *'drip and suck'* with 15ml water given every half hour and the tube aspirated before the next lot to make sure the stomach was absorbing the fluid. A very strict input-output check was kept, with twenty-four-hour tables filled in to monitor the patient's progress.

Some nights there would be a patient who had to be *'specialled'* requiring a nurse to be with them at all times making and recording observations and keeping them comfortable – usually this meant they had undergone major surgery or were coming to the end of their life. We always tried to provide comfort as much as it was in our power to do so. On one occasion an elderly man with trigeminal neuritis (pain surrounding the main facial nerve) was in a lot of discomfort and I warmed a piece of beige blanket to wrap around his head and left him sitting in a chair in his beige dressing gown while I went to make him a cup of tea. As I returned it struck me how much he resembled a large, unhappy, abandoned teddy bear. Many years later I came to know for myself how miserable and painful any form of neuritis can be.

Our first meal break of the night was at 11.45pm when the Senior Nurse took the night report to the Night Superintendent's office in the Front Hall. To allow for this journey, the first break was fifteen minutes longer than the second and third breaks. The

Night Superintendent had an odd sense of humour. One Halloween night she made strange noises on one of the half-landings, pretending to be a ghost and causing consternation amongst the juniors. Fortunately Senior Nurses remembered her doing the same in previous years and were able to restore calm. We usually spent our break times reading the previous day's newspapers and doing the crosswords. I remember one night a few of us having a prolonged debate about an article on black magic, which was very prevalent at the time. A colleague who had not been paying attention to the conversation but was irritated at the length of it asked in exasperation how long we could go on discussing a box of chocolates!

Night nurses were responsible for the patients' charts, which were kept in their folder of notes. Records of temperature, pulse and respiration (TPR) blood pressure and fluids all had to be kept up to date, and moment-by-moment fluid charts were kept on a clipboard at the foot of the bed. At first this involved much time-consuming duplication but towards the end of our training the much simpler Kardex system was adopted and did away with the copying of data from books to notes. All patients had their TPR and bowel movements checked twice daily, the latter established by the simple question: "yes or no?" Patients needed to be assisted on and off bedpans, which were metal and kept on a warmed rack. As the heating system frequently failed, we often had to run them under hot water to warm them up, being very careful not to make them too hot! There were special covers for used bedpans and urinals and woe betide nurses caught carrying one uncovered. Running taps and whistling were supposed to encourage those who could not 'go' – in my experience this had more effect on the nurses' bladders than the patients'!

Early one morning a gentleman with chest problems who used the dreaded sputum mug with great frequency produced something that resembled his uvula. My colleague decided that the best course of action was to send it to the path lab. Two days later a histology report informed us that it was "marmalade peel – probably *Chivers*." Red faces all round! Sometimes using one's initiative can backfire.

Another night, in the four-bed room furthest from the office, all the bells rang at once and we ran down there to find the place in uproar. One extremely agitated man was insisting that there was something in his bed making a noise. Earlier in the night a first-year nurse had lost her hearing aid and it appeared the man had, inadvertently, found it. The more he moved around the more it buzzed! To get the men to settle down we had to provide tea and biscuits all round – we wanted them all asleep before Sister arrived. If she had asked them what the matter was we would have had a lot of explaining to do!

Some of the men in single rooms liked to have their daily blanket bath done during the night. That way they could enjoy a leisurely bath and a chat instead of a rushed one done by the busy day-staff during the morning. This was highly irregular – we were not supposed to disturb patients – but if they were awake and they asked we would do it after Sister had made her rounds. The timing did not always work out. On one occasion Sister crept into a room flashing her torch and found a man sitting, waiting, who asked her to tell the nurses he was ready for his bath now! We hovered outside the door, cringing in anticipation of a major ticking-off, but fortunately she put it down to the patient being 'confused'. We smiled and left it at that! Another night a man asked to be bathed as he was feeling very uncomfortable. Two hours after his wash and cup of tea he died in a very neat and tidy state. Night Sister had to come up to confirm the death, which was not totally unexpected, and commented on how nice he looked. Nurses nodded in a non-committal fashion and agreed.

When a Jewish gentleman died early in the evening, according to tradition a male relative – in this case his nephew – was sent to sit with him all night as a *shomerim*. The nephew was quite a young man and the experience of spending the night alone in a mortuary became all too much for him around 2am when the hospital was very still and quiet and he was surrounded by settling corpses. The outside entrance to the morgue was locked and the lift was down in the basement, unsummonable because its door had been left open. He was trapped! There was, however, a phone and he dialled what he thought was the number of the ward his uncle had come from. Actually it was a completely different ward and the nurse on duty who knew nothing about any of this was startled to hear a fraught voice saying: "I'm in the mortuary – get me out of here!" Once the porters had investigated and freed the young man, both he and the nurse soon recovered from their fright.

It was perhaps fortunate that this did not happen on the night of the fire. Old files and newspapers were stored in the hospital basement, which was also a quiet place to go for a cigarette. One night the whole lot began to smoulder causing a lot of smoke and we had an influx of muscular firemen, much to the interest of the nurses who, since there was no danger to them or their patients, watched from the ward balconies. The water to fight the fire was taken from the lily ponds and, in the morning, the poor fish were found lying on their sides gasping in the few puddles remaining. The ponds were soon refilled and the fish revived.

Some of the 'dilemmas' faced then seem unbelievable today. In the early hours of one morning the telephone on a female Surgical Ward rang. This ward was very close to the corridor that led to the accommodation of the Senior Nursing Staff and there was a request from one of them for a sanitary towel to be taken to her flat. Back in the sixties this was far from straightforward. Should a sterile one be taken, or one out of the packet being prepared for the autoclave? How should it be carried? In those days everything was carried on a tray, but should it be in a kidney dish or a bowl? With or without a lid? I cannot now remember what decisions we came to but there was considerable serious debate on the subject before a nurse was at last despatched to deliver the article to the person caught unprepared!

Around that time two new drugs were making headline news. One was the contraceptive pill, first prescribed in 1961 and hailed as the most significant medical advance of the twentieth century, playing a major role in the liberation of women. The other was thalidomide, an anti-nausea and sedative drug introduced as a sleeping pill and then used to combat morning sickness in pregnant women. It had just become apparent that it could pass the placental barrier and cause terrible abnormalities in the babies. I remember reading about this in the papers during night duty and how horrified we nurses were that a drug could have such appalling side-effects. It was eventually withdrawn in 1962, and the disaster prompted many countries to introduce tougher testing and licensing laws for drugs.

It was while on night duty that we were able to follow the progress of a Staff Nurse colleague's pregnancy. Although she was a senior and fully trained nurse, we knew her well, as she was on permanent night duty. She was booked in to have the baby at Queen Charlotte's Hospital, next door to the Royal Masonic or, as we said, "just over the back fence". One night we came on duty to very bad news. The baby had been born, and she had cuddled it, but had then had to go to Theatre to have the afterbirth removed. While under anaesthetic she had vomited and inhaled, causing her death. The nurses were all very subdued that night.

If it seems that this chapter has been predominantly about death, this is because, in hospital as elsewhere, most deaths occur at night. Night time is when many people – especially the ill and troubled – are at their lowest ebb. Night duty was often a time to lend a listening ear to people's worries, to give reassurance and a cup of tea, and often this was sufficient to enable them to sleep. How frequently this happens in today's understaffed, performance-driven NHS I wouldn't like to say.

*

During our training we spent periods of time gaining first-hand experience in various specialties including Casualty, Paediatrics and Operating Theatre – the first two at other hospitals. St Georges Hospital opened at Hyde Park Corner in 1733, with the 'new' training building completed in 1844. We spent six weeks there working in the Casualty and Outpatients Departments. This involved travelling on the Tube in our unflattering hospital coats and hats with our caps in wicker gondola baskets. On the return journey along Ravenscourt Park from the tube station in the winter of 1961 we were often blinded by the awful smog and had to stay on course by holding onto the fence, with the street lights just visible as a very faint yellow glow. We were told that it had been far worse back in the 50s.

The most common complaint at St George's was a nail through the foot of a labourer from a local worksite. Wellies do not offer much in the way of protection and employers in those days did not provide safety footwear for their staff. Perpetual wearing of wellies does not make for good foot hygiene either – never have I encountered such filthy, smelly feet. Most doctors in Casualty wore white Theatre boots with the name of the department written on the heels in red. Going home on the tube I remember seeing a tramp wearing a pair of white boots with 'Casualty' written on them and wondering which doctor was looking for them!

The Psychiatric Outpatient Clinic was in a dilapidated outbuilding round the corner from the main hospital and reached by means of a rickety staircase. It was a dark, depressing place not calculated to lift anyone's mood and it contained the ECT or Electro-Convulsive Therapy Clinic. Patients had metal callipers attached to their heads and I hated seeing them convulse when the current was switched on and witnessing their disorientation when they came out of the anaesthetic. Years later I was to have first-hand experience of this particular treatment; it helped me but it did not help everyone.

Once in Outpatients a gentleman gave me a urine sample in a scent bottle with a very narrow neck and just a fine hole at the top. I was intrigued as to how he had got the sample into the bottle, but rather horrified when he told me he had used his wife's insulin syringe and needle. This was long before the day of single-use, disposable syringes; they were boiled up and reused!

The hospital was very close to Buckingham Palace and one evening we enjoyed lovely strawberry tarts and chocolate éclairs and were told that they were left-overs from a Royal Garden Party and we thought they had been handed over the garden wall for us. On a very quiet Sunday morning, a colleague was sitting in reception reading when a lady in a headscarf came in with a paper under her arm. The nurse looked up and said, "Can I help you, darling?" (She called everyone, 'darling'.) The lady under the scarf turned out to be Matron of St George's! Not long after this, nurses from the Masonic Hospital were sent elsewhere for their Casualty experience – we often wondered if there was a link – but at least it wasn't the Queen!

Life wasn't all fun and games, though. Caring for a docker with glandular fever I contracted the disease myself and, at the same time, managed to slip a lumbar disc moving a large wicker pharmacy basket. Following this I spent many weeks in the Orthopaedic Ward back at the Masonic Hospital, having traction for my back and antibiotics for the glandular fever. Traction was a very unpleasant experience and I was given a little teddy bear – 'Thread Bear' to keep me company. There was another nurse in the single room opposite who was also in traction – we would call out to each other when the ward was quiet and turn our radios up when a good song came on. The Brook Brothers' *Ain't gonna wash for a week!* had special meaning for us because in those days patients were kept spotless and washed continually and relentlessly – or so it seemed. My favourite song, though, was *Walking Back to Happiness* by Helen Shapiro. The muscles in my right leg had wasted and were several inches in diameter smaller than my left, and the song gave me confidence that I would be able to walk again.

It was a monotonous existence spending days on end with my bed tipped up and weights on pulleys attached to my legs with straps and bandages, and it gave me a valuable insight into how the patients felt.

Friends would visit whenever they could but my only outings were to the Hospital Chapel for the afternoon service, pushed down the corridors with my weights swaying! At one of these services we sang a hymn which has as the chorus some words from the Bible, found in Paul's second letter to Timothy: *"For I know Whom I have believed and am persuaded that He is able to keep that which I have committed unto Him..."* My situation had given me a lot of thinking time and it seemed that everything I had ever learned and known about Jesus, how He had died to free me from my sins and then risen to life again, led up to this point. It was then that I decided to trust my life and future to Jesus, no matter how things turned out for me.

Weeks later I was finally allowed up and could start exercising but my back was still very painful so I went to Kings College Hospital to have a plaster jacket fitted. I then resembled the Michelin Man for six more weeks, after which it was cut off with a saw and some alarmingly big cutters. I then wore a surgical corset with two metal rods supporting my spine and, three to four months after the injury, returned to nursing duties, though I never went back to St George's. It was this incident and its prolonged aftermath that delayed me taking my final exams. St George's

Hospital closed at Hyde Park Corner in 1981 and relocated to Tooting. The original building is now the Lanesborough Hotel.

*

Victoria Children's Hospital, Tite Street, had once been the home of Oscar Wilde, then a school, and finally a hospital. It felt very much like a Dickensian building, and closed in 1964. I gained my paediatric experience there on the Cadogan and Annie Zunz Wards. In the early twentieth century many London hospitals had an Annie Zunz Ward – she was the Irish wife of Siegfried Rudolf Zunz, a London-based German iron merchant who, inconsolable at her death, set up a trust to give grants to local hospitals that named a ward after her. To get there we walked from Sloane Square Station past the Royal Hospital, home of the Chelsea Pensioners where one evening I was invited inside to see the RHS flower show.

When two of the girls introduced themselves to the Sister she was not remotely impressed by the double-barrelled name of Student Nurse Barnet-Higgins. Snorting derisively she turned to the next in line – my friend Sue, whose surname happens to be Eardley-Stiff. An even bigger snort followed and throughout the placement she insisted on calling them both Twistington-Higgins! Cadogan Ward saw a series of children admitted every week to have their tonsils and adenoids removed and Sister dreaded auburn-haired little boys, who she said "bled like stuck pigs".

One little boy called Neville had broken his left leg and was in gallows splints – a traction device that effectively hung him up by both feet with his backside just off the mattress. As his mother was heavily pregnant he was visited most evenings by his grandmother, who wore a beautiful fur coat, and the boy would wriggle himself into position so he could snuggle into it. Neville's grandmother was Vivien Leigh.

Specialty experience seemed to be a hazardous business for me. During our placement at the Victoria, we had to do some night duty, sitting in the middle of the ward where we could see and hear all the children. The desk was illuminated by an elderly angle-poise lamp and the day before I was due to begin night duty I wanted to make sure it worked so I picked it up with my fingers curled under the base and switched it on with my right forefinger. At once a current of electricity flew up my arms and around the metal rods in the surgical corset, throwing me to the ground. The lamp was still in my hands and a colleague had to drag it away using the legs of a wooden chair. Sent back to the Nurses Home in a taxi I was afraid to turn off my bedside light and my friend had to come in to do it for me. To this day I am very conscious of the dangers of electricity. When I returned to the ward, the old lamp had been disposed of, but the scars of the burns on my finger and back took many years to fade, and the memory never has.

*

I was in my third year by the time I was allocated Theatre experience and I did not enjoy it very much. The first operation I saw was a leg amputation and all was going well until the amputated leg was put into a bucket, whereupon it fell out and went slithering across the floor leaving a trail of blood and ending up under the swab rack. A porter retrieved and removed it rapidly, while I swallowed and tried very hard not to be sick! Mastoid operations were often performed in the early sixties (the mastoid process is a part of the skull). The head was positioned with red sandbags to keep it still and the instruments used resembled a carpenter's tool-bag of saws hammers and chisels. I hated seeing the head shuddering under the impact of the hammer

and chisel, although it was only being tapped
lightly.

We had to learn the names of all the surgical
instruments and how to lay them out on the
trolley. Having to 'scrub up' and assist the
surgeon by handing him those instruments
was scary, as some were kinder to student
nurses than others. We all hoped to work for
Sir Arthur Porritt, who, if he anticipated we
might not know the name of a more obscure
instrument, would point to what he required
and say, "Please would you pass me..."

During surgery he would occasionally speak
of taking part in the 1924 Paris Olympics as a
young man, where he won a bronze medal
behind Harold Abrahams in the *Chariots of
Fire* race, and his current involvement in the
medical support of the UK Team. He always
thanked us profusely at the end. President of
the Royal College of Surgeons and surgeon to
the Queen, he returned to his native New
Zealand to be Governor General in 1967.

One of the gynae surgeons was not so easy
to work for. He liked to have the Bible read
whilst he was operating and would sometimes
stop surgery, walk over to the side table where
the Bible was laid out with a green Theatre
cloth on it, and turn the pages over with sterile
forceps to find the passage he wanted. I
remember him as a man full of his own

importance with a commanding presence and a loud voice.

All gauze swabs were counted out on the trolley before surgery began and the number written on a blackboard. When the surgeon had finished with one it would be thrown into a wheeled bowl on the floor. Sometimes they missed and we would have to pick them up with forceps, but they all ended up hung on the used swab rack in groups of five. Before the patient was sewn up they were counted to ensure none were left inside, as were the instruments.

The tension was always high in Theatre and I never felt confident or relaxed while working there. I liked my patients to be awake so I much preferred working in the anaesthetic room, waiting with them and reassuring them while assisting the anaesthetist and getting to understand the Boyles Anaesthetic Machine with its clicks and hissing. The student nurses' days ended with cleaning the Theatre. All of the marble walls had to be washed using mops on long handles and when we reached the clock somebody always made a comment about not being prepared to work 'over time'. We thought we were very clever and funny but all student nurses probably said exactly the same thing!

Chapter Four

My parents had friends who lived in Cheshunt,
Hertfordshire, having moved there from the
Isle of Wight after the war. In the early months
of 1960 I used to visit them on the Green Line
bus that chugged its way out into the suburbs
from Shepherds Bush. Their daughter had
recently left Cheshunt Secondary Modern
School but still sometimes went back for their
Saturday night dances. She and I were there
the night Cliff Richard, who was also a former-
pupil, had been invited to perform. I remember
it was very crowded with most of the youth of
Hertfordshire attending and we danced
dreamily to many of his early hits, such as
Living Doll, Travelling Light and *Teenager in
Love*.

When the primroses were in flower on the
Isle of Wight my mother picked them and
made little bunches which she wrapped in
damp cotton wool, packed in a Clarke's
shoebox and posted to me. They arrived in
good shape and were a lovely reminder of
home, but things did not always end so well.
On one occasion I was summoned to the
Shepherds Bush Parcel Depot and met by an
extremely irate man who was threatening me
with all sorts of dire penalties. My cousin, Sue,
had posted some Blue Grass perfume to me

for my birthday, the glass bottle had broken in transit and the perfume leaked out onto an adjacent parcel of game. The birds were quite inedible and their recipient very angry. It was, so the irate man told me, a punishable offence to contaminate Her Majesty's mail! As it turned out, I wasn't clapped in irons, but he refused to dispose of the parcel for me so I had to take it on the bus, enveloped in an overpowering fug of Blue Grass.

On many a day off I caught the number 27 bus to Teddington Park to visit some other friends of the family. Though I knew them as Aunty Gwen and Uncle Bill they were no relation; Bill and my father had met during the war when Bill wanted to get his wife and young son, John, out of London. Passes were eventually obtained for them to come and stay with us at Seaview, and this marked the beginning of a friendship that endures to this day. Every year they came to stay with us for two weeks in September and then, after Christmas we would go to London to stay with them and visit either a pantomime or the circus – my first ever pantomime was Peter Pan starring Margaret Lockwood. In the summer they would often take us to Chessington Zoo or to Epsom Races and we always went for a walk in Bushy Park to see the deer. It was lovely for me to be able to see them during my training and enjoy some family life.

Their younger daughter, Gillian, though still at school, often managed to be 'off sick' on the days I visited; she enjoyed hearing my stories about the hospital. Age-wise I fell between John and the older daughter, Sally. She was often out with her athletics team but when we were all together we would reminisce about the things we got up to as children, such as the time we entered the Ryde Children's Carnival, John dressed up as a fisherman, pushing me dressed as a mermaid on the base of an old pram with a notice saying *My Catch off Ryde Pier*! Sally went as a Dutch girl and Gillian as a little blonde, musical fairy.

Gwen was very welcoming and went out of her way to make me feel at home, buying me things she knew I liked, such as winkles. We had often enjoyed them on the Isle of Wight for Saturday tea, teasing them out of their shells with a pin and on one visit she made sure I had a dish of them all to myself. There was another guest that day, a very pretty and sophisticated young lady, and I felt very much the 'country cousin' de-shelling my winkles but I still enjoyed every mouthful! Most Saturdays, Gwen would make a delicious steak and kidney pudding for lunch and she always insisted on walking to the bus stop to see me on my way. It made me smile because the other end I had to walk along Chiswick High Road and Goldhawk Road on my own, where there would often be inebriated men falling out of the Raven Pub as I hurried past.

As I became more confident I found sixties London a good place to spend my off-duty time. That same number 27 bus took me to Richmond to enjoy the shops and the river or to Kew for a walk in the gardens. In Richmond was Mr Raymond Teasy Weasy's hair salon where I had my waist-length hair cut as I progressed from the white overalls into the blue dress. When we were off duty in the afternoon we could often get our hair done there for half price if we let the apprentices use us as models: it was the era when 'flyaway' hair was fashionable and Sister's comments in my report were often about untidy hair! More worrying was the time I was on the upper deck of a bus with two other nurses, one of whom was demonstrating rather too realistically how a patient of hers had been choking. The man in front just happened to be a third-year medical student and was there in a flash with his penknife ready to perform an emergency tracheotomy!

We were expected to behave in a 'seemly' manner whilst off duty and standards were high. Once when we went to watch the Boat

Race from the Furnival Gardens we were seen by Assistant Matron eating ice-creams and worried for days that we might be called to the office to explain ourselves. Another time it was hot chestnuts after a show in the West End. Free tickets to West End shows were often sent to the hospital two or three days prior to the performance and given to the staff. We also went to the cinema and saw matinee premieres of *Guns of Navarone* and the first James Bond film, *Dr No*. If off duty on a Saturday night, we might go dancing at the Castle Ballroom in Richmond, Hammersmith Palais, the Lyceum Ballroom, or to dances held at the Nurses Home. If we had just a little money left at the end of the month, there was always the Irish Club, where some of the men would be in their wellies!

Gran Wheeler's 80th Birthday party

Preparing for Ryde Children's Carnival
September 1951
L-R: Gillian Thomson, John Thomson, Dee
Roberts, Sally Thomson

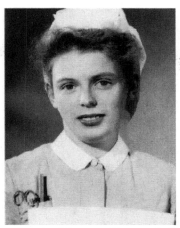

My first day in blue uniform, July 1960

Carol singing in Trafalgar Square 1960
L-R: Sue Eardley-Stiff, Denise Brightmore,
Santa, Dee Roberts, Dee Ward

Every Tuesday evening a Nurses Christian Fellowship met in the Chapel after we came off duty. Margaret, a third-year nurse, introduced me and I became a long-term member. Sometimes when we had speakers we joined with Christian midwives from our neighbours, Queen Charlotte's Hospital.   Sunday afternoons the Methodist minister Lord Donald Soper could be heard at Speakers' Corner, Marble Arch or Tower Hill. A well-known pacifist who attacked capitalism, the arms trade, blood sports and child labour, he was adept at putting down hecklers and listening to him provided interesting and free entertainment. If we were off duty by 4.30 on a Sunday afternoon we would hurry to catch the 94 bus to get to Langham Place by 6pm for the service at All Souls Church. John Stott, the leader of the Worldwide Evangelical Movement, officiated there and we needed to be early to get our favourite seats in the front row of the balcony because the church was always full. We had to be careful not to knock hymnals and prayer books off of the edge and onto the heads of those below! There was a strong evangelical emphasis at All Souls as well as support for overseas missions. After the services – sometimes midweek as well – we would gather in the crypt for discussion and refreshments.

I had my first foreign holiday in 1962 when I went with another student nurse, also called Dee, to Cattolica in Italy. We journeyed across Europe by train with £19 spending money each, taking nearly two days to reach Rimini. I remember one train was really old, with wooden slatted seats. On the way we met four male pharmacy students, also from London, whose friendship protected us from too much pestering by Italian youths – or 'Italian gods' as they thought themselves! On the first day they asked us what we did and my friend told them we worked in a fish paste factory! They looked dubious and asked what exactly we did."Oh, we make Salmon and Shrimp paste," she replied, nodding towards me. "She heads the shrimps and I tail them!"

We had a lovely fortnight in the Italian sunshine. It was during this holiday that I discovered toasted cheese and ham sandwiches and cappuccino, and we learned how to bargain for souvenirs and avoid numerous men asking, "Want to buy a watch?"! We managed to keep up the fish-paste-factory charade until we finally said good bye to our new friends on Victoria Station, when we admitted to being student nurses. "We knew it!" they said in unison.

Every Christmas I joined others going to Trafalgar Square to sing carols and have my photo taken with Father Christmas. The square would be full of happy people thronging around the enormous Christmas tree sent, then as now, from the people of Norway. Sometimes we went on New Year's Eve as well, dodging the pigeons, singing and dancing but not jumping in the fountains!

During 1961 it was decided that nurses' salaries would be paid directly into their bank accounts. As I didn't have a bank account, only an Abbey National Savings Book, I had to make an appointment to see the manager of the Hammersmith branch of the National Westminster Bank. It was quite a formal affair; he sat behind an enormous desk asking if I could give assurance that I would be a reliable client. At least the money would be paid in regularly, even if it wasn't much!

Towards the end of training I moved out of the Nurses Home to live with three other nurses and a physiotherapy student on the first floor of a large Victorian Villa. Our landlady, an elderly invalid, lived downstairs in her own self-contained area and liked to call us in to chat with her as she spent much of her day in bed. Upstairs we had a large living/dining area and there were two double bedrooms and one single at the back, which was mine. The kitchen was antiquated but we did have a separate bathroom and toilet. Both winters I was there the pipes froze for long periods of time so washing was sometimes done with water out of our hot-water bottles complete with bits of red rubber.

There was no central heating in the flat but my bedroom had a very old gas fire which I could light if I was brave enough to endure the hissing and popping. It was difficult to hold in the button and strike a match at the same time and felt rather like lighting the gas mantle in my Gran's little cottage a decade before! The hospital wasn't far to walk but the snow and ice made it slow going. There were two other flats near ours that were rented by nurses so several groups of us were heading for the back entrance at the same time. We had to travel in mufti and then change into uniform before going on duty, so 'dressing' time had to be factored into our routine.

Despite all of this I was thrilled to be 'living out' and headed for a little shop on Chiswick High Road to buy sheets and pillowcases. Since I didn't have enough money to buy two pairs of sheets at nineteen shillings and eleven-pence a pack the sales lady kindly split a pack for me. That gave me three sheets so that I could wash the bottom one each week, put 'top to bottom' and have a clean one on top (no fitted sheets or duvets in those days!) Some nurses who lived out 'borrowed' two sheets from their ward linen cupboard each week and returned their used ones to the billy bags to be laundered for them. This was fairly common practice in many hospitals but they would have been in a lot of trouble if found out. I really didn't fancy sleeping in hospital sheets, knowing what they were often soaked, smeared or otherwise contaminated with!

We rented a black and white television but there was little time to watch it. Most weekends we had a get-together in our flat or went out if we had the energy to get dressed up and put on our dancing shoes. I remember looking at two new dresses in the Kings Road and not being able to decide which one to buy. In the end I calculated that if I didn't go to the Egg and Bacon Grill that Saturday I could afford both of them! One was white with pink and mauve flowers; the other was striped in pink, grey and white. Both had full skirts worn over a net petticoat starched in sugar water.

In those days we had some boyfriends who owned an old hearse. It was rather temperamental but it got us out and about. As there were no seats in the back the passengers sat on the floor and got flung about during abrupt cornering. One of the places we frequented was the Hole in the Wall Café at the new terminal of Heathrow Airport; the roof gardens on the Queen's Building were a popular vantage point from which to watch the airplanes take off and land.

One evening when we did nothing else but watch television was Saturday November 23rd 1963, the day reports of John Kennedy's assassination the previous day reached the UK. I can quite clearly recall having just come off duty and gone to the kitchen to make a drink when the news came on. From then on we sat around the set drinking tea, unable to believe it had really happened.

It was expected that, after a year of general Staff Nursing, the next step was midwifery Parts I and II. To have any chance of promotion in the sixties both qualifications were desirable, so at the end of 1963 I started applying to do midwifery training. I was accepted by Southampton Maternity Unit, attached to the General Hospital, commencing in June 1964. I had my plans worked out – I would complete this necessary phase of my career and then return to London and work on a Surgical Ward. Before I left, the Unit held a party for me. As was customary, there was a bottle of champagne and everyone put their initials on the cork. I kept it for years.

Becoming a Midwife

Chapter Five

I headed south in the summer of 1964 with two friends, both named Sue, all of us keen to begin our midwifery training at Southampton General. We arrived with a large case each and were shown to our rooms on the ground floor of the Nurses Home – a very old building in the hospital grounds. We had to get used to 'living in' again after our years of freedom in the Evelyn Road flat! The cooking facilities here were antiquated but at least all our food would be supplied for several more months. Uniform-wise we were back to thick white overalls, brown tights and black shoes, though these did not have to be lace-ups. I had already purchased my *'Margaret Myles Textbook for Midwives'*. Always referred to as 'Maggie Myles' she was Principal Tutor at the Simpson Memorial Maternity Pavilion, Edinburgh and very highly respected in the 1960's. She played an active role on the Central Midwives Board, spoke often at midwifery seminars and her book had become the 'bible' for pupil midwives.

There were twelve students in our set, one of whom lived in the Nurses Home with the Sues and myself, the other eight lived in staff accommodation elsewhere. Most of us had come from London teaching hospitals. We found our Midwifery Tutor very pleasant as we accustomed ourselves to studying once more. Our first two weeks were spent in the classroom getting to grips with the anatomy and physiology of the female reproductive system. We would be sitting our first written exam, Midwifery Part 1, at the end of six months and had to pass this before we could proceed to study for Part II. Part 1 was entirely hospital-based, while Part II was three months in the hospital and three months on the district with a Community Midwife.

We started by practising on dolls with the callipers used to determine the head circumference of the baby – the dolls were also used in conjunction with a model pelvis to demonstrate the descent of the foetal head during labour. During the first six months there were frequent Consultant lectures at which attendance was compulsory whether we were on or off duty. These usually took place between nine and ten in the morning or six and seven in the evening. How much we took in at a 9am lecture following a night on duty was debatable! We had to gain experience, night and day, in all the different departments – Antenatal, Labour Ward, Postnatal, and SCBU (Special Care Baby Unit), as well as at the Antenatal and Postnatal Clinics.

Introduction to real-life births happened gradually, and we were taken to the Delivery Room to witness ten normal deliveries before going on to scrubbed cases wearing masks, sterile gowns and gloves, with a qualified midwife there to guide our hands and take over if necessary. My first three cases were with a midwife named Mary Wallis – known as Wee Wal, or Wallie, because of her short stature. She was very kind and encouraging, both to me and to the prospective mothers and went on to be a Sister at Great Ormond Street Hospital (GOSH). Years later I met up with her when transferring babies to GOSH for surgery and was able to reassure the parents that I knew and could highly recommend the Sister looking after their child.

The Maternity Unit was run by the Midwifery Superintendent and her Deputy, but the whole site was the responsibility of the Hospital Matron. She often took her dog for walks around the grounds and it would run ahead of her giving a very convenient warning of her approach! The dog was at her side when she performed a reading during the Christmas Production: "If there were sheep and donkeys in the stable, dogs would surely be welcome," she said. It was certainly welcome to sleep under her desk – perfectly acceptable in the sixties! – but while the dog could do no wrong, we felt that Matron was always looking for something to complain about in the Midwifery Unit.

Infection control was a very high priority. Every Monday all the staff had to take a nasal and throat swab to test for staphylococcus aureus and streptococcus and a positive result was treated immediately. Every morning two large jugs of soap solution were prepared in the Sterilising Room of the Labour Ward. The green soap came in a semi-solid state and had to be dissolved in water – we would stand stirring the jugs with large wooden spatulas as they stood on the boiling sterilisers, often reciting, "hubble, bubble, toilet trouble"!

Nearly every woman admitted was awarded the OBE – Oil, Bath and Enema! They had to force down a large measure of castor oil mixed with orange juice and a pinch of bicarbonate of soda to make it fizz; some heaved and others swallowed it down without batting an eyelid. The bath was an opportunity to relax, but many Asian ladies did not want to take their trousers off to get in. On one occasion things progressed so rapidly I had to undo the ties around an Asian lady's ankle and deliver the baby down her trouser leg as she laid in the bath. I suppose you could call that a water birth! Two hours after the oil came the enema, the instructions for which were 'high, hot and a hell of a lot'! though this was often modified in practice.

Pain relief in labour was either a Pethedine injection or gas and air. At that time episiotomies or tears to the perineum were sewn up by a Houseman or GP, though later midwives repaired these themselves. Mothers not wishing to breast feed were given a course of Stilboestrol to dry up the milk but in reality it only delayed it until the tablets ran out. For those who did wish to breast feed, milk stout and Guinness were used to boost the milk supply!

The umbilical cord was cleaned several times a day and Ster-Zac powder applied to avoid infection. It was clamped at birth, and then a sterile elastic band was put on when the baby was washed – the idea being that the band would contract as the cord dried out. This was done with two pairs of forceps and was a tricky manoeuvre needing much practice to get right. Cotton cord ligatures were also used, and later cord clamps were brought in which were much easier to apply, but not all innovations were as welcome. When I began midwifery the mothers brought in four name tapes – two with a female name embroidered in pink and two with a male name in blue. After the birth the midwife would sew whichever was appropriate round the baby's wrist and ankle. Some mothers wrote on the tapes, some left them blank or forgot to bring them so the midwife would make them up herself before threading the massive needles with the red thread provided. Sometimes a colleague had to hold the baby's limbs still for safety's sake while the labels were sewn on but the 'modern' plastic bracelets that replaced them were hard and rough and rubbed the baby's delicate skin – especially those that were overdue.

If the delivery rooms had been busy sometimes there would be a backlog of two or three babies waiting in a warm bathroom to be washed and dressed. Here we checked them for 'clicky hips' and gave them an injection of Konakion to prevent Vitamin K Deficiency Bleeding – newborns can easily lack vitamin K since it does not easily cross the placental barrier from mother to child. I remember once being very surprised at the strong smell of spices in the room and learning that spices eaten during pregnancy crossed the placental barrier very easily and came out in the babies' skin and breath! The mothers also brought a pink nappy pin and a blue nappy pin to fasten the hospital terry nappy. We always made sure the boys were 'pointing downhill' or else we might well find the gown and sheet sopping wet and the nappy bone dry!

After giving birth, the mums had a wash and a cup of tea and were taken to the Postnatal Ward, their babies in cots at the sides of their beds during the day but taken out at night. The babies wore little shirts, the arms ending in mittens taped at the wrist to stop them scratching their faces. The shirts had ties at the back and were tucked up to avoid them getting wet. Occasionally they wore hand knitted bootees for warmth but these had to be regularly and closely inspected to make sure there were no loops of wool inside. There had been a case, written up in a midwifery journal, where a baby had lost a toe because wool in its bootee had wrapped around it and cut off the blood supply leading to gangrene. Each cot had a pink or a blue label with the baby's name, date and time of delivery, and birth-weight; when the UK went metric people still preferred the weight recorded in pounds and ounces.

First-time mothers stayed for eight to ten days and all of them remained in bed for the first three and had to be swabbed twice a day – the first time by the night staff before they handed over to the day shift. Most of the four-bedded rooms had bed-curtains but, in the seven bedded rooms there were portable screens that left gaps and were prone to falling over – mothers used to joke that it was hardly worth pulling them round. Weekday mornings around 11am a physiotherapist would arrive to organise the postnatal exercises, following which the mums would lie prone (face down) to encourage the uterus to return to its normal shape and size – anteverted and anteflexed. This position can be highly uncomfortable with engorged breasts, so a pillow would be placed under the stomach to create room for them.

Some mothers were transferred to Cottage Hospitals in Hythe or Romsey and some to the Postnatal Ward at the Chest Hospital (now Southampton Western). The mothers went in wheelchairs and their babies were carried out to the waiting ambulance. One day when six or seven were being transferred at the same time two babies got mixed up and were given to the wrong mothers. It was a while before they realised they were not feeding their own babies – in 1965 little fuss was made about it; today it would cause a furore!

Babies definitely knew the scent of their own mother's milk – we did little experiments with breast pads and the babies would become excited and nuzzle into those from their own mothers while ignoring those from others. Breast feeding was not as popular in the sixties as it is now, with many people using National Formula Milk. At this time there was a milk kitchen attached to SCBU where all the formula milk was made up. It took two people all morning to wash and sterilise the bottles using the electric bottlebrush and the teats, rubbing them with salt first. Anyone who worked in the milk kitchen carried the smell of milk and Milton with them everywhere despite the gowns we wore to cover our uniforms. Special Care babies had expressed breast milk or half-strength Regal Milk. Later the manufacturers supplied us with small, ready-prepared bottles, which made life much easier.

It was relatively unusual for a baby to be a face presentation where the head becomes extended (chin up) instead of flexed (chin tucked in), but there was an occasion when I experienced two on consecutive nights. The first was the mother's second child; her membranes ruptured just before full dilation, no cord could be located and the baby, just short of eight pounds, was born with a very bruised and swollen face. As was customary he went to SCBU for 48 hours until the bruises began to subside, but he still tended to keep his head extended. Mother and baby stayed for a week, and he came back to the hospital for follow-up appointments.

The night after his birth I attended a rhesus negative mother whose third baby had been induced that afternoon. Labour was progressing well but when she achieved full dilation here was another face presentation. This one was a girl and, although she took some pushing out, she was much smaller at only five pounds ten ounces, probably due to the unhealthy placenta, and she did not look as much like a boxer on the losing side of a bout than the boy did! Both babies rested in SCBU and rejoined their mothers at the same time. The girl was rhesus negative as well so there were no blood issues; she fed well and was gaining weight when discharged.

The SCBU was on two floors – upstairs were the very small premature babies, some in incubators, most tube-fed. Each had an individual, colour-coded, rubber nasal gastric tube, measured from the bridge of the nose to the tip of the sternum and a coloured thread tied round it to indicate how far it was to be inserted. As the babies grew they were measured regularly and new tubes made. Before feeds the tubes were boiled up in the small instrument steriliser and then cleaned afterwards. Premature twins were sometimes put together in one incubator so that they would not miss each other.

In the mid sixties there was not much equipment to help in the care of these tiny babies and a lot was down to good nursing. One special little boy I named 'Boots' because he looked so cute lying in his incubator, all two pounds of him, in his blue booties. One afternoon he was quite poorly, having developed Respiratory Distress Syndrome, he looked so tiny and fragile and I so wanted him to survive. I remember standing by his incubator earnestly praying that he would grow up to be a big, strong boy. He did survive and I followed his progress until the family moved away, by which time he was a very active toddler, into everything and doing very well.

Once the 'sucking reflex' was established the mums could come up to SCBU and bottle feed their babies. Other visitors were not allowed in but could queue up at a window into the corridor on Saturday and Sunday afternoons when the babies would be held up for them to see. It was usual for one set of grandparents to come on a Saturday and the other set on a Sunday, each set convinced that the baby took after their side of the family!

From time to time a baby would be baptised while in SCBU. The Anglican Chaplain would bring his bottle of holy water and a small marble font and wooden cross would be put on top of the incubator, while the parents stood at the sides. It was always a moving and emotional service and a privilege to be part of it. After the first baptism I attended the parents went back to the ward and the vicar was recording the details so I began tidying up, emptying the font into the sink and putting the cotton wool swab into the bin. From behind me I heard a sharp intake of breath and found the vicar incensed! Holy water was not to be poured down the sink, but onto the grass outside, along with the swab! I did not let on that from time to time I had tidied up swabs left on the grass outside as I had believed they were litter and an eyesore!

If a Roman Catholic mother had a stillbirth we had to get a priest in to baptise the baby within an hour. If one was not available then a Catholic midwife was sought, but if no Catholic was on duty then anyone was permitted to baptise the baby using the name John or Mary. Some young and inexperienced priests found it very difficult when the baby had severe abnormalities. The grass outside that was blessed by the Holy water was part of a garden with a large, crescent shaped bed of azaleas and rhododendrons in the centre. It had been donated by the Rothschild family of Exbury Gardens to show their appreciation of the care given to their premature twins some years before. I especially enjoyed the garden on night duty, when I would stroll around it during my 4am break, breathing in the glorious scent of the yellow azaleas.

Back on the main Postnatal Ward the turnover of patients was fairly rapid but there was still time for delicate situations to arise. On one occasion a first-timer (known as primiparous or a *primip*) was taken into a seven bedded room that was almost full of second and third-time mums *(multips)*. Everyone was getting along well and supporting each other, and then visiting time came around with the usual influx of fathers clutching bunches of flowers. Almost at once one of them came rushing back out looking horrified – the *primip* was his girlfriend and one of the other mums was his wife! The girlfriend was swiftly moved on the pretext that it would be better for her to be with other first-timers, and the wife was transferred to the Chest Hospital the next day. Whether they found out about each other we never knew. When we weren't protecting people from their own complicated relationships we were sometimes called upon to be the bearers of good news. It was around this time that I answered the phone to a patient's husband to be asked, "Will you tell my wife that Elsie's had thirteen?" They were farmers and Elsie was their sow!

Names were another thing that could cause difficulties; did her parents really want to call their daughter Tanya Hyde? All I could think of was my mother telling me "I'll tan your hide if you don't behave!" After one of my early deliveries, the mother hadn't chosen a name for a daughter and named her Deanne after the other midwife and myself – the father was not consulted. I remember that the name Marigold was often put forward for girls but no one ever took up the suggestion! Later in my career I took a very small baby up to Great Ormond Street Hospital, handed him over and gave his name as Arthur Sydney Percival Henry. "Good Lord!" said the receiving nurse, "that's a mouthful for a little chap to cope with!"

Any baby with an abnormality however small was seen very quickly by a Paediatrician. At that time many chromosome defects were being identified and given names – often the name of the specialist who had been researching the condition. Orthopaedic conditions like clicking hips (congenital dislocating hips) and talipes (club foot) were referred to the specialist from the Children's Hospital in Winchester Road. Clicking hips were treated with double nappies unless very severe in which case a plaster of Paris splint was put on. Mild cases of talipes were gradually corrected by the mother exercising the foot. Worse cases were strapped into a better position. Breech babies often looked very cute laying with their feet up by their ears until they gradually straightened over a few days. Those with hare lips and cleft palates usually had to be spoon fed because sucking was difficult for them and for these we used a special blunt scoop-shaped spoon that slipped easily into the mouth without spilling the milk over the sides.

Whilst working on the Antenatal Ward we would attend the Antenatal Clinics at East Park Terrace down in the city. The Houseman and the Registrars would give the pupil midwives a lift in their cars, crammed in with the notes and equipment; then we would spend the morning testing urine, taking blood pressure and gaining experience of palpating. This last involved working out the position of the baby in the womb, diagnosing a breech presentation and being able to ballotte the baby's head. If the baby was still breech at 36 weeks, the Registrar would attempt to turn it. Iron and Folic Acid were often prescribed – if the mum's iron levels were very low, an intramuscular injection of Jectofer might be given. One of the clinic's more memorable patents was a school teacher who arrived for every check-up on a dropped-handlebar bicycle – including the one just seven days before her due date!

A strict watch was kept for albumen in the urine; along with oedema and a raise in blood pressure this presaged pre-eclampsia, and the mother had to come into the Antenatal Ward to rest and be regularly checked, possibly for the remainder of her pregnancy. Mums expecting twins were often brought in for bed-rest as well. It was difficult for the girls to be away from home and they would often swing from laughter to tearfulness in a minute. In those days the trumpet-shaped Pinard Stethoscope was the only way of listening to the foetal heartbeat to make sure the baby was alright, though a few years later we had the sonic aid to use alongside. If birth needed to be induced early this was done with drugs, either intravenously or by insertion of a vaginal pessary or by ARM – Artificial Rupture of the Membranes ('breaking the waters'). Alongside the mothers being induced there might be one on a Duvadilan alcohol drip to try to stop premature labour, which made them feel drunk.

When I began training mums stayed in bed for at least 48 hours but eight months on ideas had changed and they were allowed up after 24 to go to the toilet, although still encouraged to rest as much as possible. Each one was escorted to her first bath which, much like the postnatal cup of tea, was very much appreciated. It was fairly common at that time for women having their fifth or sixth baby to follow it up with a sterilisation and stay for five days. There was a small Observation and Isolation Unit with two large rooms which could be used as delivery rooms if necessary. This was a much less frantic ward to work on with two cubicles for isolating babies and a series of single rooms for mothers and babies together.

The upstairs Postnatal Ward, Rownham's, also had single rooms in which those recovering from Caesarean Sections were looked after for 48 hours. Back then we called the operation a LSCS, or Lower Segment Caesarean Section – I don't recall that we ever said *C-Section* as they do today. After two days mum and baby were moved into one of the eight-bedded rooms. This ward was more spacious than the downstairs Postnatal Ward, and was for people staying longer and requiring more nursing care following breech, forceps, Caesarean or twin deliveries. I found this ward similar to the Surgical Wards I had enjoyed back in London; there was not so much coming and going and more time to get to know mothers, help them with breast feeding and show them how to care for their babies.

Chapter Six

We were students again! We worked hard, and we played hard too. Very soon after arriving in Southampton, my Dad found me a green Fiat 600 in the second-hand car showroom at Wootton on the Isle of Wight. I went over once to view the car and then the following weekend I went back to collect it. As I hadn't yet passed my test, Dad had to come with me, but we couldn't get a crossing from Cowes to Southampton so we had to use the Yarmouth to Lymington boat. This meant I had to drive into Southampton over the Totton flyover, which was choc-a-block with holiday traffic! My 'new' little car did not take kindly to this, over heated and began to steam. I was so glad that my Dad was with me to handle the crisis and call the AA!

It was not the last time I had to call on him to sort out a motoring problem; I remember once meeting him at Southampton Pier as he arrived on the boat. One of the Sues had passed her test so she had driven down with me and after the car issue had been addressed he took us both for afternoon tea at the Cadena Cafe in Above Bar Street. The tea arrived with a two-tier cake stand laden with chocolate éclairs and meringues. These were rare treats indeed for cash-strapped pupil midwives and we did not need much urging from Dad to join him in having a second one each. I knew that area well because I attended Above Bar Church on a Sunday evening whenever I could. With split duties it was difficult to get there regularly, so I more often went to the Nurses Christian Fellowship that met weekly in the Nurses Home.

When the car was working I got lots of driving practice around the local area with Sue. She had a red Mini, which was always parked next to my green Fiat – we called them Mini Lou and Feeny Fiat. Where parking was tight, if there were enough of us, we would get the nose of the Mini in approximately the right place and then adjust its positioning by lifting the rear end into the kerb! Sometimes we went to West Wellow to pay homage to Florence Nightingale who is buried there in the churchyard of St Margaret of Antioch. Often we took a picnic into the New Forest and fed the ponies at Lyndhurst (an activity much frowned upon today!) or we might go to Winchester, or Farley Mount with its downland and woodland walks. It was good to have the freedom a car brought us and be able to drive down to the Hamble River or up the Itchen Valley to look for water voles, inspired by Ratty in *The Wind in the Willows* story. I'm not sure how wildlife-friendly the river was at that time: the local saying went: "Fall in the Itchen and come out scratchin'!"

One weekday evening, around nine when it was still light, three of us took a thermos and drove to some fields at the back of Thornhill to have our coffee nightcap al fresco. We were disturbed by a helicopter circling continuously over head coming lower and lower – we could see the occupants waving at us and hear them shouting that we should pack up and go home. We could see nothing wrong with what we were doing so we took our time. Later we found that three prisoners had escaped from Winchester Prison that afternoon! Did they at first think they had located them, only to find it was three nurses having a late picnic? Another time we were out late in the wilds was when the husband of a patient who lived in the New Forest arranged to take a group of us out at dusk to see wild deer. They were far less easy to spot than escaped convicts and we circled round them so we could approach them upwind and not frighten them away. Afterwards we stumbled back to the cottage in the twilight for coffee.

I had never been to the Proms when I was working in London but a colleague was keen on classical music and wanted to go, so five of us managed to get half a day off. I drove us up to Town because I needed to practise for my test. We found a parking space very near the Albert Hall and queued with the other promenaders to hear Jacqueline du Pré play the cello. Having been in the queue for a very long time we were in the front row and able to lean on the bar and even sit on the floor until the promenade area became too full. We were alongside several music students who were very knowledgeable about the music – especially one young man the others referred to as 'Squirrel Nutkin! It wasn't until many years later when Jacqueline du Pré died that I realised what a truly celebrated musician she was.

Six months into training, after sitting Part 1 of the Midwifery Written Examination, four of us set off on holiday to Devon and Cornwall in Mini Lou, wandering from one Bed and Breakfast to another, getting out and about whenever there was a let-up in the pouring rain. We spent several nights in a hotel on the cliff-top at East Looe and one night decided to go and see a play in Looe Village Hall. It was tiny! The four of us took up a whole row. After that we went on to Polperro and stayed in a B&B beside a very noisy river in full spate. None of us got much sleep there. Later we found ourselves in a small hotel in Minehead that was effectively a care home for the elderly. Amazingly this was the second time this had happened – back in Torquay we had witnessed two elderly gentlemen nearly coming to blows over ownership of a newspaper. We could not quite work out how we had managed this trick twice.

Almost as soon as we were back from holiday it was time to start planning the Christmas entertainment – the sets above and below us now had a head start on us and had been getting themselves organised while we were away. The concert was performed in the classroom at teatime on Christmas Day, and each group did a song or a sketch, most of them based on midwifery and the various Senior Midwives. The Superintendent of Midwifery was a tall, elegant woman with silver-grey hair always worn up in a bun, and the pupil taking her off had pinned a silver wire-wool pot scourer into her own hair, which was red. It looked very comical despite often falling out. All in all it was a hilarious occasion with everyone taking part in good spirit – the Senior Midwifery Sisters were not left out and did a sketch and a song of their own. For several years a horse made of chicken wire and papier mâché called Wilberhorse also made an appearance.

*

On commencing Part Two of our training the Central Midwives Board issued each of us with a Case Book in which we had to detail the medical histories, antenatal examinations, progress of labour, drugs administered, patients' remarks, reports on puerperium (events following the birth), the baby, postnatal examinations and summaries of cases for six women delivered in hospital and six delivered at home.

Soon after Christmas the allocation list for our three-month community placements appeared. Both Sues along with myself and another girl were to be working on the East Side of the city in Thornhill, Bitterne, Sholing and Woolston so we went home-hunting. Eventually we found a semi-detached house behind the shops at the top of Bitterne Hill – perfect for the Sues and I, as the other girl was local and living at home. We moved in just before we commenced working in the district, which meant a few long bicycle rides across the city to attend lectures at the hospital, and Bitterne Hill was long and steep! At the bottom was a roundabout leading into the one-way system, manned every morning by a very large policeman known as 'Tiny' Dyer. He always called out to us on the downhill run and halted the traffic so that we could sweep round the roundabout without stopping. He was a very popular policeman – with the cyclists if not so much with the motorists! After that it was a long haul, mostly uphill, to get to our lectures. Two days before I began work in Sholing I passed my driving test and became a motorist myself.

A lot of 'my' families lived in prefabs on an estate just off the main road from Portsmouth to Southampton. They were very compact and it was easy to find things as they were all identical. The Community Midwife supervised me for the first few deliveries and then left me to it, just calling in from time to time. This was exciting and scary at the same time! Not all houses had a telephone and the mobile phone had yet to be invented. If people did have a phone it was often a shared or party line.

During the day I still rode my bicycle but at night or to attend lectures I now had the option of using my car. Travelling to a delivery on a bike with the bag strapped over the back wheel and a bedpan in the front basket was a skill that had to be perfected. It never happened to me but I heard of other midwives going over potholes at speed and the metal bedpan bouncing noisily out of the basket and down the road whereupon they had to go back and retrieve it complete with another few dents. One Sunday evening at church two midwives arrived very late because the chain on one of their bikes had come loose and fallen off – a passerby had been co-opted to help repair it. As we settled back down into the service the last hymn had a rousing chorus of *"My chains fell off, my heart was free; I rose, went forth and followed thee!"* We found ourselves totally unable to stifle our laughter.

Sue Two used a Honda scooter to get around her district, which was Thornhill. There were a number of tower blocks and even in those days it was not entirely safe to leave a bike there unattended. The day came when she exited a block of flats and the Honda had vanished, but an extensive search found it on the far side of the complex by another entrance. Had it been moved by a prankster or had she just forgotten what door she went in by? On future home visits the Honda accompanied her up in the lift, standing on its back wheel!

As there were three of us in the house, sorting out both cars and the Honda at night could be quite tricky. We tried to leave the car most likely to be needed parked last in the drive but it was not always easy to second-guess which one that would be. Some nights with all the comings and goings and rearrangement of vehicles, we wondered if the neighbours thought we were running a 'house of ill repute'! One morning two very intense

Mormons knocked at the door. We needed to get out and do our visits so we invited them back one afternoon to talk to us and were joined by a Salvationist friend of ours. It was an interesting hour with no conversions in either direction but we were highly amused when they introduced themselves as Elder Johnson and Elder Berry!

In 1965 home visits were made to new mothers twice a day for three days and then daily until the tenth day when mum and baby were handed over to the care of the Health Visitor. Mums who were discharged from hospital forty-eight hours after the birth had their care taken up by us on day three. I very much enjoyed this aspect of midwifery as it meant getting to know the whole family. Grandparents and fathers like to have something to do and many cups of tea were offered us at each house, which was fine so long as the loo was indoors.

I was also introduced to a level of poverty far below any of my previous experience – I remember once being given my tea in the only cup and saucer in the house, mismatched, chipped and cracked, while the father drank from a metal mug. It was kind of them to give me tea at all. When home conditions were like this it was considered best that the birth took place in hospital. A friend visiting a home in one of the poorest areas of the city had a narrow escape when walking along a lino-covered hallway with a small piece of carpet halfway along. Just before she got to it a voice called out "Don't tread on the mat!" It was covering broken floorboards and under it was a gaping hole into the cellar!

In Asian homes I had to get used to a different method of tea-making. A large metal jug or kettle was put on the stove with water, Ideal Milk, tea leaves and sugar in it. This mixture was then boiled up, stirred from time to time and left to simmer. The result was a very sweet milky tea, often accompanied by Asian sweetmeats. I drank this concoction politely but it was definitely 'not my cup of tea'!

As we were 'living out' we had to provide all of our own food, although our pay was still very low. Economy was the order of the day – the low point of which was end-of-month lentil soup made to a war-time recipe. I remember a time I was clearing up after an afternoon delivery when the new father came into the bedroom and asked me how long it would be before I was finished. When I told him fifteen minutes he said that supper for the three of us would be ready then – he had been out to the local butcher and bought three steaks! I have never forgotten either the mouth watering smell or the wonderful taste of that meal.

One of the Community Teaching Midwives heard about the lentil soup and began donating food to us regularly, afraid that we were not feeding ourselves properly. Whenever she made cakes she would send some along for us. We also came in for any glut of vegetables from my Dad's allotment. He would pack them in a box and send them over via the Red Funnel steamer from East Cowes to Southampton Pier – in those days it cost nothing as long as someone was at the ferry terminal to collect the box as soon as the boat berthed. While we waited we would often take a walk round the docks to look at the big liners like the Queen Elizabeth and Queen Mary. The arrival of the box was always an especially happy event when it contained strawberries!

The story of one twenty-four-hour period will give you some idea of how life was for a trainee Community Midwife at that time. Midnight brought a call-out to a second-time mum. All was straightforward and she progressed quickly with minimal pain relief, delivering an eight-pound, eight-ounce girl at 2.40am. I washed them both, cleared up and was home to bed just after 5am. At 8.30am I was woken by the phone. It was my Community Midwife saying I was to go straight away and do the morning visit for the new mum and then join her at the home of another woman in labour. When I arrived there at 10.30am I found the midwife drinking tea and playing with the toddler! Everyone was very relaxed and another baby girl arrived at 6pm weighing in at six pounds twelve ounces – a little small but the mother smoked heavily and had high antenatal blood pressure. Following the birth it was still slightly raised. After clearing up there I was glad to go home for a meal, but at 9.45pm I went back to check that all was well, especially her blood pressure.

At the end of our time on the district we had to sit our written midwifery exam. This took place in Southampton but was followed by a VIVA in London, which caused us a few sleepless nights. We practiced with the doll and model pelvis and tried to learn the names of the Obstetricians that had been put to various instruments and manoeuvres. There were the Kielland forceps for turning babies high up in the birth canal, Neville Barnes forceps for babies not progressing and Wrigleys forceps for a low lift out when the mother had become exhausted. The Mauriceau Smellie Veit manoeuvre was used in breech deliveries and the Brandt-Andrews manoeuvre for delivering the placenta. None of these names, as you can see, were particularly easy to remember, or to spell!

The VIVA was in two parts. First we had a pregnant lady to examine and take a case history; mine was a very large Jamaican woman who had numerous children, one of which had been born in a field in Jamaica. On the day of the second part I drove myself and three others into central London. We found the hall, changed into our uniforms and lined up with hundreds of other pupil midwives from all over the country, making our way gradually up a massive staircase, gradually getting nearer the hall, some of us desperate for the loo – but we had to stay in line. Eventually the large double doors opened and we filed in to find our appointed table. Behind each table sat a Consultant Obstetrician and a Senior Midwifery Tutor. The Tutor at mine sat very erect and wore a cap with a most uncomfortable-looking bow under her chin. For ten minutes they took it in turns to ask me questions.

I didn't find the experience too stressful but I did hope that I had got the Jamaican lady's story accurate. Being so large she had been difficult to palpate but I thought the baby was presenting by the breech and when I had said so she had given me a knowing grin that made me almost sure I was correct. After the exam we changed back into our mufti and went to visit some old nurse friends from the Masonic Hospital in their flat. Then we had a long and awful drive back to Southampton in the driving rain, despite the fact that it was summer.

We had enjoyed living in Bitterne but our tenancy at the house there was up and we had to find somewhere nearer the hospital. Four midwives who had been in the set above ours told the Sues and me about a vacant flat in the house where they lived. It was in Bassett Row off The Avenue – a very up-market address, with five self-contained flats and a sweeping staircase. The vacant flat was in the attic, full of character and very spacious. We loved it on sight and it was great to be living near other midwives with whom we often shared meals and trips out, taking it in turn to drive down to Above Bar Church on a Sunday evening.

It was at this time that I joined the Navigators, an American-based evangelical and discipleship outreach working in UK hospitals and universities. Their Bible studies and TMS (Topical Memory System) were a great help to me, with a new verse to be learned every week from a range of themed Scriptures. Our leaders were not always that understanding if the verses had not been well-learnt! Many of those verses I still know today, but there have been so many new translations of the Bible since then that they tend to muddle themselves together in my mind, so the one I come out with is 'the translation according to Dee'!

Chapter Seven

After the exams were over we treated ourselves
to a fortnight's holiday and then it was back to
the hospital for Staff Midwife experience, more
responsibility and cases involving the new
intake of students. I enjoyed this aspect of the
job very much, especially working on the
Labour or the upstairs Postnatal Wards. The
Labour Ward was quite small and cramped,
having two large delivery rooms and one with
two tables, two admission rooms and various
bathrooms. The three first-stage rooms all had
two beds and no privacy whatsoever, with just
a curtain between them. The Antenatal Ward
was next door and the Antenatal Midwife
would often come in and help at night. Most of
the incidents I recall most clearly happened
while on night duty.

One night the bell went from a toilet situated
between the two wards. This was unusual and
I hurried round to find that the light had fused
and a patient was sitting there in the dark. As
I switched on the light in the bathroom next
door, the woman said very calmly: "I think my
baby has been born." Peering between her legs
I saw the baby boy, who had fortunately been
a breech presentation, sitting in the toilet bowl
looking up at me! (My second water birth?) The
woman had thought she was "just a bit
constipated." Given the amount of care usually

taken with breech births it was amazing that it turned out so well. The baby spent 24 hours in SCBU and was given antibiotics as a precaution but neither he nor the mother was any the worse for the experience.

This happened on a night when we were not too busy, but many nights were frantic – birth, like death, often occurs during the hours of darkness. It was not unusual to have all the delivery rooms occupied and one night Sue and I found ourselves in the smallest first-stage room, both our mums progressing well, both using gas and air and both having had babies before (*multips*) so we all knew they would be delivering where they were. The baby on my side of the curtain had just been born when I heard Sue's voice saying: "Dee, do you think you could get your mum to move her foot from my sterile trolley?" Concentrating on the 'business end' I had not noticed that a foot had strayed through the gap in the curtains and was resting in a large, formerly sterile, kidney dish!

A woman who has had five or more babies is known as a *grand multip* and we had one arrive in the early hours of the morning in an advanced state of labour with a breech presentation. We just about managed to get her into a delivery room and one leg up in the stirrup when the Houseman did very little more than catch the baby as it emerged. The mother, who was clearly quite a character, vowed in the most colourful of language that she would not let her husband get her that drunk again and the whole event was accompanied by many expletives and much marital abuse!

Another emergency took rather longer to deal with and considerably more input from me. I was examining a girl whose waters had just broken with some force and found a large pulsating loop of cord in danger of being constricted by the baby's head. Calling for help, I managed to get her onto all fours and the Houseman and Registrar arrived to find me holding the baby's head up from the cord so that the blood flow was not cut off to the rest of it. The Theatre in the General Hospital was alerted and we embarked on a mad dash along the corridor with me half sitting on the trolley maintaining the pressure to keep the head in the right position. It was just as well that it was the middle of the night! Up the steep incline to the Theatre we went, closely followed by the Paediatrician and SCBU Sister with the Resuscitaire – a neonatal warming and resuscitation machine. I had to stay as I was for what seemed like an eternity; my wrist and arm were aching badly but I knew I couldn't alter my position without risking harm to the baby. At last, to the great relief of everyone, the baby was safely born, responded well to the ministrations of the Paediatrician and was taken back to SCBU for observation.

To aid the midwives, each department had a team of Auxiliary Nurses and a Ward Orderly who served drinks at night and helped with cleaning and other work. These were wonderful people, most of whom had children of their own and understood first-hand how the patients were feeling, and we could not have managed without them. One Orderly I especially remember was not a great conversationalist. She would push her night-drinks trolley into each ward with a clatter and call out: "'Ot or cold?" which meant in effect: "Would you prefer hot or cold milk?" She would then pour the drinks and bustle away without further remark.

The Isolation and Observation Ward on the first floor was not a prison, but one family went to some trouble to 'spring' mother and baby in the middle of the night. We found them gone the next morning with a note of explanation left on the bedside table saying the father was coming at 2am to take them home. Spelling was not the mother's strong point and she had asked other mums for help, getting a different one to spell each word so no one could work out what she was planning!

They made their clandestine exit down the fire escape to what we at first thought had been a pony and trap, but it turned out to be a lorry.

Southampton's population of Afro-Caribbeans was fast increasing at this period of the mid-sixties. One night a Caribbean Islander who had only recently made the journey to Britain was brought in quite early on and, as the contractions grew stronger, she began to sing a calypso, clicking her fingers and toes as she did so: *"Oh, Lordy, take this pain away or I ain't gonna love You no more"*! The idea of singing and concentrating on the song during a contraction was very popular with first-time mums who had been to antenatal classes, though the British weren't quite so creative or heartfelt and tended to go for *Ten Green Bottles* or *Old MacDonald had a Farm.* The words might have been easy to remember while in pain but it did become rather repetitive for the midwives. Towards the end of one long night I recall walking out of a delivery room and saying to a colleague "If those damn green bottles don't all fall soon I will scream!"

In all my years working on a Labour Ward the same coded phrase was always used to indicate that a cup of tea had been made. Someone would call out "Mrs Brown is fully!" and we would hurry off to tend to the fictional

Mrs Brown, who was fully-dilated, and get our cuppa. Nowadays when I watch television programmes such as *One Born Every Minute* and see the midwives gather around the tea trolley and then go running in response to a bell it takes me back to my experience of doing exactly the same thing four decades and more before.

In 1968 two government departments merged to form the Department of Health and Social Security. During the first week of the merger the Southampton Ambulance Service received a call to a home in the poorest part of the town and arrived to find a man, obviously healthy, who instructed them to take him to draw his benefit. When told in no uncertain terms that this was not the job of the Ambulance Service he said: "Yes it is; you're now the Department of Health *and* Social Security!" He seemed to think this entitled him to free transport each week to collect his benefit.

In the outlying villages, the annual fetes were always very popular, with all the traditional attractions: dog shows, flower arranging, bands, stalls and sideshows and of course a bonny baby competition. The Maternity Unit was often asked to provide two midwives to judge the baby show and, since the Senior Midwives were all wise to the hazards of such a job, they took very good care to have prior engagements on that day that prevented them from attending! So one Saturday – persuaded by the concession that it counted as 'on-duty' time – Sue and I in our smart uniforms went to a village called Hedge End to provide our expert opinions.

Prizes were to be awarded for the 'best' girl and boy. We decided that we would check the two fontanels (soft spots on top of the head) of each baby and then just go for the most appealing. We did try hard to make everyone feel special by admiring a feature of each baby, but having made our choices, and at the same time made enemies of every other parent in the competition, we were grateful to get away without being chased by an angry mob! After this traumatic experience we vowed we would never get inveigled into judging a baby show again. Fortunately the custom gradually died out, though there are some recent signs of it re-emerging.

Off-duty time came at a premium as we often stayed to deliver a mum we had been with all day rather than hand her over to a stranger, and even when the delivery was over there was still a lot of paperwork to complete – the certificate for the Registrar of Births, two registers, the mother's notes and the baby's notes. So we made the most of the free time we had to go out and about and a favourite place to walk was round the docks with the hulls of the big liners towering above us. There was no restricted access in those days and they looked massive and majestic – even more so as they made their way up Southampton Water past the Western Shore and Netley.

After some time, one of the Sues left to join the Naval Nursing Service, which meant the two of us remaining could no longer afford our spacious flat in Bassett and had to look for something smaller. For a while we stayed with other midwives then at last found a flat in Shirley, just as we were going away for two weeks holiday. To save us paying the rent for those two weeks a colleague offered to store some of our belongings for us. She lived at home and her parents were agreeable, so a lot of our things went into their shed and the rest went into an unused rabbit hutch! It was an unconventional storage unit but it saved us a lot of money.

When we came back from our holiday we moved into our new home where we had the use of the ground floor of a semi-detached house comprising a sitting room, bedroom and kitchen. The toilet was outside and the bathroom was upstairs where the owners lived – we were permitted two baths a week as long as they were not too deep! Short on furniture we got two sturdy orange boxes from a fruiterer in Shirley High Street, covered them in material from the market and converted them into a coffee table and bedside cabinet. Our bedroom had French windows onto the back garden and when we were off duty on summer Sundays, two till four, we would open them, sit on our beds and listen to the play on the radio. We called these our sanatorium afternoons.

For our TV, we went to Radio Rentals where Sue threw me completely by giving her name as Miss D Roberts. This left me no choice but to give hers – Miss S Eardley-Stiff, which always had to be spelled out, letter by letter including the hyphen. When we got outside and I asked why she'd done it she said: "Oh I just got fed up with my surname!" I could completely understand that, but it didn't mean I wanted to swap! To this day, Sue has a wonderful, mischievous sense of humour. She eventually moved to take up a Community Midwifery post in Portsmouth, and trained to become a Health Visitor. We have remained firm friends and, now we are both retired, we enjoy holidaying together again.

Of course Sue's departure meant that I had to find new accommodation again and, after a short spell in a flat provided by the Navigators I moved in with Paulina and Janet in a spacious but rather cold house in Swaythling. It turned out to be a time for new beginnings all round. I saw a Sister's post being advertised within the Maternity Unit, applied for it and was duly promoted. A new role with more responsibility beckoned!

Chapter Eight

I had a whole new uniform to go with my
'elevated status'. Firstly a dark blue long-
sleeved dress with stiff detachable cuffs which
were only worn when the sleeves were down –
there were frilly cuffs to go around the sleeves
when they were rolled up. It was essential that
we did not leave our wards without rolling
down our sleeves and attaching the stiff cuffs,
though finding our own sometimes proved
difficult! The dress collar, also detachable and
very stiffly starched, was held in place with
studs that rubbed the back of my neck. Most
Sisters had a hospital buckle on their belt that
was worn with as much pride as was the
hospital badge. Soon after promotion it was
customary to go to a photographer and have a
very serious studio portrait done – you can see
mine at the beginning of the book!

We Sisters ate in a secluded dining room
where we were served rather than queuing up.
Each of us had a linen napkin for which we
had to purchase our own, individually-
recognisable napkin ring. It was very scary the
first time I embarked on the long walk up the
corridor to the general hospital, clutching my
napkin ring, and ventured into the dining
room. Matron and senior staff had their own
table, General Ward Sisters were next along
and Maternity Unit Sisters sat near the

kitchen. On entering we collected our napkin
from the sideboard and went to sit at the
appropriate table, beautifully laid with a
damask cloth, quality cutlery and glasses. I
was convinced that, at the very least, I would
spill my meal down my front and make a
spectacle of myself! The Midwifery Sister Tutor
had grapes for her dessert, served on a plate
with a pair of small scissors and a gorgeous
cut-glass finger bowl. As I watched her
delicately cut off a few grapes to eat and then
dabble her fingers in the bowl I could not help
but remember the kitchen flannel that was
produced to wipe sticky fingers in my
childhood!

A less formal occasion was Sisters' Coffee.
This happened after the Consultant and
Registrar rounds had been completed and all
the other staff had their breaks, in the SCBU
office, which was a large room with plenty of
chairs and a toaster. Leaving the Houseman to
handle discharges and the Paediatricians to
examine the babies (with the aid of a pupil
midwife to dress and undress them) we would
all rush to the office, desperate for a drink.
One of the orderlies would have provided a
trolley laden with mugs, coffee and tea, but
was not around to ask us "'Ot or cold?" as she
had long since gone home to bed! It was
Sisters' Coffee that gave me a taste for toast

with Marmite *and* Sandwich Spread, a delicacy I was introduced to by a fellow Masonic nurse on the first morning.

This was an era of great medical advances when people were inspired to experiment in ways that would not be tolerated in these risk-averse times. The first heart transplant operation was performed in South Africa by Christian Barnard, but unfortunately the medication given to the patient suppressed his natural ability to fight infection and he died from double pneumonia. If that had happened today, would the life-saving transplant program have been halted in its tracks? Some aspects of human nature never change, though. Back in the autumn of 1967 there had been a strike at the docks which had lasted several weeks and led to power cuts and much national upheaval. How do people occupy their time when there is no work and no power? Nine months later we found out, as the Maternity Unit was stretched to breaking point!

There was one patient whom I will never forget, a sixteen-year old single girl who had gone through a difficult and prolonged labour culminating in a Caesarean Section. She came into Rownham's in a very exhausted state, still having IV blood and very slowly began to get over the trauma, only to develop an infection and be put into isolation in one of the single rooms. Her parents had been very supportive but it had been decided that the baby, still in SCBU, was to be adopted. One day I found a beautifully wrapped box with a ribbon bow on her bedside table. As she was understandably very low and unhappy I tried to persuade her to open this present, thinking maybe it was something to distract her and cheer her up, but she refused. Over the next two days I made several more attempts but the present remained intact.

It was still there when I helped her to pack her things ready to go home, so I put it on top with the sparkly bow sticking out. Later that morning her mother arrived to collect her and I went into the room to give them her discharge notes. To my surprise they gave me the gift I had been trying so hard to get her to open. I unwrapped it there and then and found a Royal Albert, bone china coffee cup and saucer in a pink rose design, filled with chocolate mints. The accompanying card said: *"Thank you for being so kind."*
I often wonder what happened to that family and if mother and child have ever been reunited. Now I am downsizing and trying to minimise my clutter but I can never bring myself to send that particular cup-and-saucer set to the charity shop.

The old days when there had been 'children' and then 'adults' were gone – this was the age of the teenager, with sixteen-year-old Twiggy a supermodel, actress and singer, appearing on the covers of Vogue and Tatler. During my time at Southampton the youngest girl I cared for was just thirteen and the oldest woman fifty-two. One lady I remember was having her first baby in her early forties. She had been a businesswoman and found the bonding process very difficult. "I know I need to talk to the baby," she said, "but I feel so stupid because I know he doesn't understand." I suggested nursery rhymes but she felt even sillier reciting *Ba-ba Black Sheep*. My next idea – fairy stories – was better received and soon the tale of Red Riding Hood could be heard emanating from her private room. Gradually she got the hang of caring for her baby – I wonder if Red Riding Hood was always his favourite story? Hopefully his grandmother did not have big teeth!

Day duty on SCBU occasionally meant a trip up to Great Ormond Street accompanying a baby being transferred there. Every morning, both in SCBU and on the Labour Ward, the 'Flying Squad' equipment would be checked to make sure it was all in order should it be needed. Great attention was paid to the slightest detail, as lives might depend on it and a Paediatrician was always in attendance. We had to ensure that a bed at GOSH was available, our team complete and ready for the journey, the parents fully informed and the police alerted to organise an escort for us. The baby in the portable incubator, plus equipment, would then be loaded into an ambulance and off we went.

The M3 had not yet been built so we would make our way up the A30 through all the little towns and villages – this was why we needed our police escort to smooth the way for us. There was a bridge at Bagshot where traffic filtered left for Windsor and our original escort departed. On my first GOSH run I remember the lights were red and in front of us was a group of motor bikes, all with pillion riders, their feet on the ground as they waited for the green light. The ambulance driver edged forward and the motorcyclist must have looked in his mirror and seen us because he moved out of our way. Unfortunately the pillion rider didn't notice and was left standing, still in the astride position, with the bike gone! He became aware of the absence of the bike when he fell over in the road!

As we approached London we were picked up by a second police escort – outriders on motorcycles – who effortlessly cleared us a path through the traffic. That first baby I escorted was going to have an exomphalos – a large portion of bowel lying outside of the abdominal wall – repaired. He was relatively stable and needed little attention during the journey but a baby could very quickly and unexpectedly deteriorate if not watched carefully. Once we had handed him over we had refreshments in the GOSH canteen before returning home rather more slowly and with no police.

On the second occasion I made the trip the baby was much sicker, having been born with a diaphragmatic hernia where the contents of the abdomen were pushed through the diaphragm into the chest cavity inhibiting the functioning of the lungs. Many checks were made before leaving Southampton with the baby intubated and two Paediatricians in attendance. All was going well until we reached the outskirts of Hartney Witney when it became necessary to re-intubate. We got the driver to pull over into a lay-by and I handed the laryngoscope to the Paediatric Registrar, only to find that the light integral to the instrument was very dim – and that changing the battery produced very little improvement. The movement of the ambulance had caused the batteries to run down during the journey.

What could we do? The baby's life depended on getting him re-intubated quickly. I prayed, looked out of the ambulance window and suddenly noticed we were parked near a small general store and in the window was a sign that said: *"Ever Ready Batteries"*. The ambulance technician was out of the cab, over to the shop and back with the necessary batteries in seconds. I am convinced that it was no coincidence that we stopped in that lay-by, but a 'God-incidence' that the notice was right in front of me when I glanced up. Very quickly the intubated baby 'pinked up' and we continued our journey, the police escort again joining us to see us safely through London. On this occasion after he was safely bestowed, the crew felt they had earned more than a snack in the canteen and we all headed for a café they knew. The doctors took off their white coats and the ambulance men's uniform was fine but I felt very self-conscious eating out in mine! Since I had no money on me I got a free meal out of the Ambulance Service that evening. The café staff naturally wanted to know all about our journey but patient confidentiality prevailed and their curiosity went unsatisfied.

A fellow Sister, friend and former neighbour had artistic talent and had drawn a series of midwifery-themed cartoons, which she had submitted with some success to the Midwives Chronicle, a monthly professional journal. One

I particularly liked was of tiny twins lying in an incubator, one with a speech bubble saying: *"Here comes the midwife"* and the other saying: *"Go on, hold your breath – it really scares them!"* How true that was!

Around this time advances were being made in neonatal care and a lot more was being understood about jaundice and how it was caused by too much bilirubin in the blood, which the immature liver was unable to break down. Bilirubin is a pigment found in bile and, when a phial of blood was left by accident for eight hours on a windowsill, it was found to have significantly less bilirubin than a fresh sample. Often babies would be found sunbathing in front of south-facing windows and further research led to phototherapy lamps being a standard form of treatment for neonatal jaundice, with pads held in place by elastic web bandages to protect newborn eyes.

Most relationships with mums and families were unavoidably transient – we knew them for a brief dramatic period in their lives and then no more. There were times, however, when a longer involvement was possible. During one spell on the Antenatal Ward I cared for three mothers all expecting twins and became friendly with two of the families, visiting them at home and invited to the babies' Christenings. It was very interesting to see the continuing development of the children and to see which of the characteristics they had at birth were retained. The twin who had been placid and easy to feed in the incubator remained so; the unsettled difficult one was always picky with food.

Paulina and Janet were promoted soon after I was, and then it was my turn to instruct them in the intricacies of Sisterly etiquette, as my friend, Liz, had once instructed me! It had become necessary for us to move out of our house because the landlord had other plans for it, and we had heard about a flat that was coming up for rent, close to Southampton Common and The Dell stadium – in those days the home of Southampton Football Club. It was an attic apartment that had recently been done up and newly equipped and we loved it – it was so warm! Each bedroom was full of quirky features and there were new kidney-shaped dressing tables provided with flower-print curtain skirts – it was all so pretty and feminine compared to the antiquated dark wood in our previous house.

We needed a fourth midwife to share and soon Mary, who had just come up from London, joined us. After we moved in we found that the beautiful red carpet in the hall and stairs actually took rather a lot of effort to keep clean. The toilet was fine for us girls but we derived great amusement when visiting men tried to use it – after the seat was lifted up it remained in place for precisely two seconds and then fell down. The resulting expletives could be heard in the sitting room.

A more universally appreciated benefit was the garden, which we had the freedom to enjoy without having to maintain it, and where we often picnicked with friends. At the bottom was stabling for several horses with a disabled foal called Nadia. She suffered from a degree of spasticity following a difficult birth and was allowed to wander at will, always coming to us to be petted as we went to and from our cars. One morning I found her asleep in the downstairs hall with her head resting on the first stair! She must have come in early with the postman.

The Free Church Hospital Chaplain in the late sixties was the minister of Swaythling Baptist Church. Since there were very few young people in his congregation he said he would be grateful for our support so we began to attend there. During the following months we got to know the minister's family quite well and were invited for tea from time to time. Once we were interrupted by a shriek from the downstairs cloakroom, whereupon the mother jumped up saying: "Oh dear, she's fallen down the loo again!" Sure enough, their two-year-old daughter was found stuck with her legs up by her head looking for all the world like a breech baby!

There were always groups of midwives going up to concerts in London. Once, on returning to Janet's Mini parked in a Kensington side road, we found that it had been broken into and, along with a sandwich left on the dashboard, a bag containing her uniform had been stolen. Of course she didn't want to lose her hospital buckle and badge and we thought the thief might have discarded the bag when he found no money in it, so we began to hunt around the surrounding streets. All the houses seemed to have small gardens and steps leading down to basement flats, so it was no easy job in the dark. We had walked a long way and were just about to give up when we spotted the bag in some bushes – amazingly the uniform was there intact, complete with belt buckle and badge, though the sandwich had been eaten and the wrapper discarded.

I always enjoyed working nights. We had a Night Superintendent in charge when she was on duty but on her nights off I would often be the Senior Midwife. One of the most enjoyable aspects was doing scrubbed deliveries with new pupil midwives – they were always so excited and apprehensive at the same time. Those first deliveries were so important to the

students – most midwives always remember
who supervised their first scrubbed delivery –
and often a bond would form between midwife
and pupil.

Training underwent a great change when the
Integrated Midwifery System was introduced.
It was no longer in two parts with exams after
each, and community experience came much
earlier. After a number of pilot schemes up
and down the country, Southampton moved to
Integrated Training in 1968. Four pupils who
joined that set were Ann, Lizzie, Dibs and
Rene. Ann was one student with whom I did
scrubbed cases. She was finding training
difficult, as her engagement had been broken
off and she spent a lot of time in our flat where
she could make phone-calls in peace and
privacy. In the end she returned to general
nursing in London but, years later, her
daughter trained to be a midwife and went on
to have a pivotal role in setting up and
running an inner-city Unit supporting teenage
mothers.

When the time came for them to do their
community experience one of the first calls
was in the middle of the night. Everyone got
up to help Rene get off to the delivery as fast
as possible. She had very long hair that she
usually wore pinned up but to save time the
others encouraged her just to pile it up on top

of her head and hold it in place with her midwives' hat. When she arrived at the home, the GP told her: "No need to stand on ceremony here; take your hat off!" The hat was removed and Rene's hair cascaded down over her face leaving her completely sightless!

Breech and twin births were usually shared around to give everyone experience of less usual deliveries, though of course ultrasound scans were still in the future, as were tests for Down Syndrome, and any abnormalities came very much as a shock to all concerned. Most nights passed in a sort of routine busyness but we always had to expect the unexpected and sometimes the rare and unusual cases came in clusters.

A third-time mother in labour with twins was taking everything in her stride at first, moved to the delivery room in plenty of time with the Obstetric Registrar and the Paediatric Team on hand as usual. The first baby was breech and there was a nice, controlled delivery of legs and trunk before everything became stuck. There before us was the little-seen complication of locked twins, where the second twin's head was below the head of the one already half-born, preventing it from emerging. The skill of the Registrar enabled the second twin's head to be moved so that both babies could be born, though the first

one needed resuscitating. He responded well
after a few tense minutes and was despatched
to SCBU with his sibling for forty-eight hours
observation. I went off duty wondering if I
would ever see locked twins again in my
career. At that time there was a one-in-eighty
chance of conceiving twins but locked twins
were very rare indeed.

Back on duty the following evening I found
another mum labouring with twins – this time
she was a *primip* which was likely to make
things more difficult – but by ten-thirty
everyone was in place as before. It was with a
strong sense of déjà vu I saw that the first
baby was again, breech presentation and
astoundingly the twins again became locked.
On this occasion a different Registrar had to
perform the difficult manoeuvre to free the
heads. Both babies responded well eventually
but needed a longer time in SCBU to recover.
These were the only two instances of locked
twins I ever saw and they came sixteen hours
apart! Four live babies was a wonderful
outcome – only a few years before it would
almost certainly have been a more tragic story.

One night a mother and father arrived with
their eighteen-year-old daughter clearly in
labour. Until forty-five minutes previously they
had no idea she was pregnant – she had
known but been too scared to tell them. They

were in a state of shock, the mother repeating that she couldn't believe she hadn't noticed. The baby was safely delivered and home they all went. Four weeks later the same couple turned up with daughter number two – exactly the same thing had happened! This time shock gave way to angry disbelief, the reluctant grandmother distraught at so quickly facing the identical embarrassment all over again.

It was a far less busy night when we were enjoying a cup of tea while the rain and wind lashed at the windows when a middle-aged man ran in, dripping and dishevelled: "My wife's in the car!" he said. "She just woke me up and told me to bring her here!"

"Is she pregnant?" I asked.

"I don't think so...!" was the somewhat baffling reply.

I grabbed an umbrella and wheel chair and hurried out to the car park. As I opened the door of the car I heard the lady inside making an unmistakeable noise: "There's only one time in her life when a lady makes that noise!" I told the husband. "You are in the right place!"

The couple were both in their mid forties and, once I had her on the bed I could see why they might be confused – her stomach was flat and she certainly didn't look pregnant. My colleague and I feared we would deliver a tiny foetus incapable of sustaining life but, very quickly, a five-and-a-half pound baby was born. The mother had felt no movement throughout, had believed she was menopausal and visited her GP the previous week complaining of excessive indigestion! Once he had got over the shock her husband was very pleased and went home to wake his son and daughter, both around twenty, to break the news to them. Just before I went off duty in the morning they all returned to see the new addition to the family – apparently it had taken him some time to convince his older offspring that he was not joking!

In the summer of 1968, after much lobbying by the Sisters, the Superintendent of the Maternity Unit made the decision that we could wear short-sleeved, white polycotton dresses, instead of our old-fashioned, long-sleeved, thick, navy ones. Even though we had to buy and launder them ourselves we were so much more comfortable and they would drip dry over the bath in a few hours and require no ironing. Starch was a thing of the past!

Christmas decorations at Southampton Hospital were not quite as elaborate as those in London but we still enjoyed planning them. By that time the old red rubber mattress protectors had been replaced by disposable polythene ones that went under the draw sheets. We found we could make pretty Christmas wreaths with these if we cut the polythene into strips one inch by nine and tied them onto wire coat hangers bent into a circle. A few strands of tinsel and a bauble hung in the centre completed the design – cheap but somewhat labour-intensive! Mums were still kept in hospital for ten days, post-delivery, so we co-opted them to help with the Christmas project. Other cheap decorations included baubles made of old Christmas cards cut into circles, folded and stapled. They went up a couple of days before Christmas and came down again around the 28th December; they could not be up too long, in the interests of infection control.

On an evening a few days before Christmas there was a Sisters' supper party, to which we all arrived with big hair and short dresses! I remember Mary making her red dress herself, especially for the occasion, but my needlework skills were not up to that standard. Christmas morning every baby received the gift of a pair of bootees. These were knitted by volunteers – many of them by my Mum. A special frilled skirt was put around the cot of the first baby born that day and the ward was visited by Father Christmas and the Mayor, accompanied by local press photographers.

All that year we had been closely following the preparations for the launching of the new liner QEII. Turbine difficulties had led to the postponement of her maiden voyage but eventually all the teething troubles were sorted out and she arrived in Southampton ready for a big send-off on May 2nd 1969. The night before, the docks were thronged with well-wishers, everyone wanting to get a glimpse of the majestic ship – the Queen and Prince Philip came that night as well. The next day when she sailed every inch of shoreline down Southampton Water was packed with flag-waving, clapping, cheering people.

Being a port, it was not unusual to have babies born on board vessels out in the channel, and mother and baby would then be transferred to us by ambulance to be checked over. It was not easy to discern exactly where the birth had occurred, and this was important to know because the waters in which the baby had been born determined where it had to be registered. Often this required a journey to London by the father.

In July 1969 there was great excitement over the anticipated moon landing. I remember sitting up with Janet watching our flickering black-and-white television as Apollo 11 touched down on the lunar surface and Neil Armstrong first set foot on it. An estimated five hundred million people worldwide saw this moment and heard the famous quote: "That's one small step for man, one giant leap for mankind!"

In many ways this was a time of great hope and optimism, with the war receding behind us and a new era of scientific progress and personal freedom begun. In London, the Hanson family had the first set of quintuplets to survive in the UK and the first of the Isle of Wight festivals celebrated the burgeoning music industry and young people making their own way and their own rules. But under the surface gloss, people were still experiencing the same problems and weaknesses that no amount of science and social change can address.

One morning a pupil midwife failed to arrive for work. She lived in hospital accommodation just up the road and her housemates remembered seeing her at home the night before. Eventually someone was sent to the house to look for her and was horrified to find her dead in her bed. It transpired that she had died of an overdose of sleeping tablets – many bottles were found in her room, some came from the hospital in London where she had worked before; all of them had patients' names on them. A growing dependence on these drugs had led to her taking them from the medicine cupboards and her death was most likely entirely accidental – she had just swallowed too many. Much stricter checks were introduced to make it more difficult for staff to help themselves to medication.

In the autumn of 1969 I was back on Rownham's Ward working with a slightly older pupil midwife whose parents had recently died. She and her brother were finding life rather difficult and feeling that they were just drifting along with no purpose. When I asked her if she would like to help me sort out a nativity scene for the ward at Christmas, she jumped at the chance and became very motivated, taking trips to London to buy figures, oxen, sheep and donkeys. Her brother was happy to make the stable, complete with manger, and fitted a light to shed a soft yellow glow for atmosphere. Both of them really enjoyed creating the nativity, which turned out a much grander affair than I had first envisaged, and it was put on display a few days before Christmas. So sturdily made was it that it moved with me to be used in four different locations over the next twenty-five years! During this time I added a number of wooden animals, which I bought while on visits to Bethlehem. These unbreakable figures were good to have as the children could play with them and rearrange them to their liking.

In the mid-sixties the Salmon Report was published setting out recommendations for developing the structure of nursing staff and the status of the profession in hospital management. In practice this took some time to filter down to Maternity Units. Two pilot schemes were set up at opposite ends of the country – one in Sunderland and one in Southampton, with the intention that we should meet up and compare progress. The distance between us made it difficult but it was essential that this should happen, as there were no computer communications between hospitals at this time. Gradually the role of the midwife expanded to include things previously done by the Houseman. Much of the routine work had been taught to each new Houseman by the midwives anyway!

Through this process a link was made with Newcastle Hospital and we at Southampton became a Teaching Unit for medical students. We shared a number of Obstetric Registrars and Housemen, including the Professor of Obstetrics and Gynaecology. Many of the doctors commuted between Newcastle and Southampton, as by this time some motorways were being built, including the M3 from London to Southampton. One Registrar returning south at night crashed just outside the city and remained in a critical condition for many days. Before going for convalescence he came to visit us in the Labour Ward and we hardly recognised him, so bruised was his face.

Every five years each midwife had to attend a residential refresher course and, as I had qualified in 1965, mine came round in the spring of 1970. The Midwifery Superintendent was keen for me to do mine at Durham so that I could make contact with our Sunderland partners and maybe visit their Maternity Unit. Being away from home for a whole week caused great difficulties for those married with children, but my only inconvenience was the long train journey north – and the fares were paid. The visit to the Sunderland Maternity Unit was very interesting – it was fun to meet and chat with other midwives about training and recruitment, but our time together was limited. The refresher course delegates stayed on the university campus and I found the lectures and visits very interesting, but some older midwives resented these compulsory courses and sat at the back of the hall knitting and chatting throughout!

It was customary for qualified staff to transfer from their training hospitals and gain experience in different Units and in various parts of the country and, not long after the refresher course, Mary and I decided to move on from Southampton. My initial plans of hurrying back to London and working on a Surgical Ward had somehow evaporated. We saw an advert placed by the council of Harlow in Essex, wanting young professionals to join in setting up the new town. It sounded like an exciting venture to get involved in – quite different to practising in a large port city like Southampton. We applied to the Princess Alexandra Hospital, had interviews and were accepted, moving to Essex in the beginning of October. Most of my household belongings were shipped home to the Isle of Wight to be stored until I needed them again.

Indian-themed Christmas 1963 (that's me
kneeling far right)

Before going to the Sisters' Christmas Supper
Party
L-R: Mary Manley, Dee Roberts, Paulina
Symons, Janet Vince

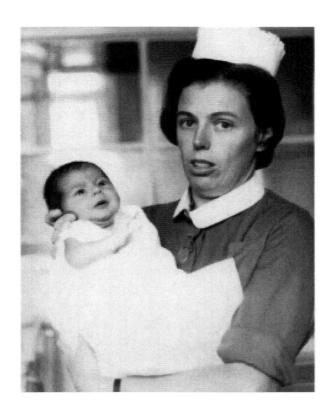

Not long after becoming a Midwifery Sister at
Southampton

Harlow

Chapter Nine

In my little car, packed with our belongings, Mary and I made our way up to London, round the North Circular and then along the A414 through Hatfield and Hertford to Harlow. It felt like a long, slow journey but eventually we arrived at Princess Alexandra Hospital and were shown to our rooms in Christiansund House. All the residential blocks were named after Norwegian towns and, forty years later, I actually visited some of them on a cruise, but for now Bergen, Oslo, Narvik and Stavanger were buildings.

On reflection, October was probably not the best time to move. Essex seemed very cold – the east wind blew straight across from Siberia and I very quickly bought myself a fur bonnet. I missed Southampton and found it difficult to adjust. Christiansund housed only Sisters and Charge Nurses. It was very modern and comfortable – a great improvement on staff accommodation in Southampton – but I was used to seeing people I knew when I was out and about. Here I knew no one.

Harlow Council gave young professionals like us priority on their housing lists and we decided to move out of the hospital as soon as possible. In the meantime the two of us joined

Old Harlow Baptist Church and made some new friends there. The Minister and his wife had three young girls, nearly always dressed in red with red ribbons in their hair. They were very welcoming towards us – most of the rest of the fellowship was considerably older and they were glad to have some people nearer their own age.

The Maternity Unit was a new, single-storey building joined to the General Hospital. It was not as busy as the one at Southampton but it did have a lot more modern facilities. There was a Unit adjacent where GPs and Community Midwives could come in and care for the families and, if more was required, the women could easily be transferred to Consultant care. All the rooms in both departments were spacious with curtains around each of the four beds. There were also some single rooms, one of which held the decompression chamber – a huge contraption that looked similar to an iron lung. There was a theory that it reduced the discomfort of contractions but I never saw it used in the two-and-a-half years I spent at Harlow. Nowadays they feature in the treatment of various conditions but not, so far as I know, in childbirth.

One particular midwife, Betty, was very supportive and helpful to us new girls. Not

long before, she had walked into a theatre
light positioned low in a delivery room and her
face was terribly bruised. The aneurysm would
heal and the bruising subside only for it to
break out again and again. Lights and lighting
were a hot topic at the time as this was the era
of strikes, the three-day week and power cuts.
Again, nine months later, we were
overwhelmed with the results of people having
to provide their own entertainment! Since
there was nothing anyone could do about the
situation and we were all in the same boat, we
developed something of a blitz mentality and
just got on with things as best we could,
working around the difficulties.

One bright spot in these difficult days was
Ann's wedding, which took place in Kidbrook
in London. Mary and I were thrilled to be
invited and drove up together. During the
reception there was a power-cut and we found
that the venue had made no provision
whatsoever for this common occurrence –
Ann's brother had to go out and find some
camping lamps. Afterwards we had a hair-
raising journey back to Harlow with all the
traffic lights out!

Early in 1971 the Council offered us a
maisonette. It was a lengthy walk from the
hospital, the decor was all dark brown and, at
the top of the stairs, a life-sized tiger had been

painted on the wall, poised to spring at anyone coming up! We declined that one. The second one we were offered was in The Stow, a village-like area of Harlow with its own shops, library and village hall near to the park. This maisonette was above the Council's Neighbourhood Office and we quickly agreed to this one, partly because we liked it and partly because the previous tenants had been a Midwifery Sister and her husband who had left it in very good order needing nothing done to make it habitable.

As we prepared to move we were faced again with the difference in the cost of 'living out' as opposed to 'living in'. At Christiansund House, loo rolls, washing up liquid, toilet brushes, disinfectant, bleach, etc were all provided – as was the cleaner who used them. Now we had to buy all of this and more for ourselves. Near the office on the Postnatal Ward were two large walk-in cupboards, their shelves packed with a plentiful supply of all the articles we needed, and it came home independently both to me and to Mary what a massive temptation they posed for hard-up people. I hasten to add that we didn't steal anything ourselves but we understood and sympathised with those who did.

My Dad and Uncle hired a van and set out very early one Saturday morning to bring all my gear up to Essex and help install it. We had a couple of old carpets – one a lovely embossed Chinese one – and Mary had been busy making red curtains to enliven the living room. We bought a new gate-leg table, chairs and a sideboard, but had no money left for a stair carpet. This was solved by procuring two books of carpet samples from the local furniture shop and getting to work with a hammer. Each tread was carpeted in a plain colour with the riser in a co-ordinating flecked design – a very attractive effect that was commented on by nearly everyone who came to the door.

Despite all this 'nesting' activity and the approach of my 30th birthday I was becoming more and more depressed – to the point that I was soon not even able to work. With hindsight, this depression had begun before I left Southampton and now my birthday – which was also Decimalisation Day – passed me by in a fog of misery. Even buying myself new sheets and pillowcases in bright shocking pink didn't lift me for long, despite my Mum coming up to stay with me during some of the time I was off work.

The Princess Alexandra Hospital had a Psychiatric Department called the Churchill Clinic and after I had been off work for some time my GP referred me there. It was very difficult for me having to do this, not in a safely anonymous environment like most patients, but somewhere I was known. Medication just wasn't working so it was decided to admit me as an in-patient from Monday to Friday and for me to have ECT twice a week for four weeks. I still had vivid memories of watching the patients convulse as they underwent this therapy at St George's and was very anxious and fearful.

I had a single room in the Unit, for which I was very grateful, as I found the bizarre behaviour of some of the other patients quite distressing. Things did go missing, though, so I didn't keep many of my possessions in there. Once I was on my way back to my room and saw a young patient in the corridor wearing a pair of sheer tights, fluffy slippers and my turquoise sweater – a comical sight but also a sad one. I did eventually retrieve my sweater.

The day arrived for my first ECT and, unbeknownst to me, the anaesthetist on duty that morning was one the other midwives did not trust. When they saw the rota they decided they must do something about it so Betty contacted another anaesthetist who was not due in until the afternoon and she willingly came in early to give me my anaesthetic. In the end she came in with me every time to administer my anaesthetic and I was always relieved to see her; she made the experience a lot less scary.

Whilst an in-patient at the Clinic I had to go to group meetings and occupational therapy, which I quite enjoyed. During my time there I turned out many wicker baskets and trays, all made with wet willow, and I also designed and made crochet shoulder bags and waistcoats – everyone had hand-made gifts for the Christmas of 1971! Craft really helped the days go by and I am so pleased that I never lost my creativity.

These were the final days of ECT as a treatment – its effectiveness was already being questioned and it was phased out in the mid-seventies. I was warned that my memory would be affected and that there would be great gaps in what I could recall. The immediate effect was on numbers; for instance a telephone number I had used for years was suddenly gone from my head, but long-term I have very little memory of the entire two-and-a-half years I spent at Harlow, which is why this section of my memoirs is rather short on midwifery anecdotes. Good things, interesting things, heart-warming things must have happened there, but they are all lost to me.

Some things I do remember were neither good nor heart-warming. One Sunday morning Mary and I hurried out of the maisonette with very little time to get to church and found the boot and offside rear door of my car had been spray-painted with blasphemies. The black paint showed up very clearly on my pale grey-green car and I was worried it might offend the elderly members of the congregation so I parked very carefully at church – reversing into a space so that the offensive words were not visible to anyone. There were several local incidents of cars being vandalised at that time – the police investigated but got nowhere. That afternoon, with much effort, we managed to clean it all off and the church folk never knew about it.

The families at the Baptist Church were very kind, often inviting me home for meals or on trips out with them. They and Mary were very long-suffering with me but it is anything but easy living with someone undergoing depression – everyone close to them suffers along with them. I don't remember exactly how long I was sick, but it was many months. My confidence took a long time to return – especially for night duty – and I found it difficult to sleep and to adjust my medication. The Sister and Staff Nurse in the Churchill Clinic remained very supportive and I could go and talk to them whenever I needed to. They were firm with me about the need to keep moving forward and get out of the dark tunnel by changing my way of thinking. I will always be grateful for the help they gave me.

There was a Royal College of Midwives group that met in the hospital from time to time – I don't remember any such thing happening at Southampton. Community Midwives would congregate from all the local towns like Bishop Stortford, Epping and Ware. At one of these meetings someone spoke about the need for nurses and midwives to save for their retirement. This seemed a long way off at the age of thirty but I took notice and made an appointment with The Stow branch of the Norwich Union. The next week I committed to save five pounds a month with them for twenty-five years, and five pounds was a large chunk out of my salary in the 1970s, but I contributed faithfully for the rest of my professional life and now I'm very glad that I did so.

One quiet weekend one of the Registrars told us that she often pierced people's ears for them. Several midwives wanted theirs done, though I was most definitely not one of them! It was arranged that she would hold an 'ear-piercing clinic' the following afternoon in a delivery room where she could make use of the big theatre light. Mary had hers done and developed a nasty and painful infection which only served to confirm all my prejudices. It was another thirty years before I eventually had mine pierced and it was done professionally!

Although I was still on a lot of medication my anxiety was under control and my confidence was returning. On one of my days off I remember going by tube from Epping into London. At this time long tartan kilts were in fashion so I made my way to the bottom of Regents Street where there was a very large Scottish shop. It was quite narrow but went back a long way and I enjoyed pottering around, looking at all the clan tartans and reading about their origins. My father's roots were in the Campbell clan so I considered designs featuring their plaid, but in the end decided to try on a mauve, black and white tartan skirt and a Stuart dress kilt. No sooner had I got into the changing room when all the lights went out.

As it was lunchtime I realised that the power was likely to be off until at least mid-afternoon. A shop assistant brought in a hurricane lamp and I tried the clothes on in the flickering shadows, eventually deciding I preferred the mauve one. It was very eerie making my way back up the long, dark shop to pay for it! Many of the surrounding shops had closed. Having learned to crochet while in the Churchill Clinic I made myself a black waistcoat to wear over a white blouse with my new skirt and wore the outfit to the Baptist Church's New Year's Eve party and Watch Night service.

January 1973 saw Britain finally taken into what was then known as the Common Market by Edward Heath, who had relatives in Seaview and was often seen sailing off the Isle of Wight. Around then I realised that this was decision time for me as well and that I needed to move from Harlow. There were several reasons for this – I wanted a job where I wouldn't be required to do night duty; my Mum was not well and I had to be able to get back to the Isle of Wight easily. Above all I needed a fresh start. I knew I didn't want to go back to Southampton, but I did start investigating other hospitals south of London and arranged three interviews – one at St Peter's Hospital, Chertsey, one later the same day at St Luke's, Guildford, (both in Surrey) and one on another day at Northwick Park, Brent. The post at St Luke's was to be the Senior Midwife in charge of the postnatal floor, with no night duty. I was very pleased when I was offered this and I arranged to begin work there on May 1st 1973. The majority of my belongings returned once more to the Isle of Wight to be stored until I needed them again.

Settling in Surrey

Chapter Ten

Back in hospital accommodation! At Guildford I had a sitting room, bedroom and bathroom to myself but shared a kitchen across the landing. It was small but warm and comfortable and I had brought a few of my belongings to make it feel like home. My first fortnight was spent in an orientation programme, meeting people and visiting the different departments, the smaller GP Units at The Jarvis on Bellfields Estate in Guildford and St George's Wood in Hazlemere, and also the Maternity Department of Mount Alvernia, the private hospital.

St Luke's had grown out of the Guildford Union Workhouse Infirmary – the Casual Ward for tramps, known as the Spike was there. It had only closed in 1963 and, ten years later, some still turned up hoping for food. While I was there the Spike was used for storage. Normally the porters would retrieve any notes that had been deposited there but occasionally I had to collect the key and venture into the dark and cold, dodging cobwebs and mouse droppings! Thanks to a Jubilee Grant it has now been transformed into an interesting museum telling the story of life at the Spike for gentlemen of the road in times past, but

back in the 1970s many older residents
disliked St Luke's because of its history –
much like St Mary's Hospital in Newport.

I completed my orientation with a tour of the
large laundry in the grounds of Farnham
Hospital, which also served St Luke's. As I was
new to the area I was taken there by another
midwife who was just getting back into driving
after a long gap. It was an interesting visit but
I remember more about the journey than the
laundry as, at one point, we found ourselves in
the middle of a large grassy roundabout and
had to reverse off! Then it was time to make
my way from the Nurses Home through the car
parks and up the stairs, feeling once again
very much the 'new girl', and take up my role
as head of the postnatal floor.

St Catherine's Ward was quite different to
anything at Southampton or Harlow. The main
ward had twenty beds with a smaller, seven-
bedded room at the far end and a two-bedded
cubicle near the office. At the top of the stairs
were two nurseries and the hospital policy was
for the babies to remain there and be carried
out to their mothers at four-hourly intervals
for feeding. I never liked this policy; though I
recognised the problems of mothers getting
any rest with twenty babies in one room I
believed it was far better for mothers and

babies to be together. The policy did gradually change but it took many years.

On the same day as I started, so did a new Ward Maid who came from Madeira. Lydia had a big smile and very little English at first, but that soon improved. The ward was difficult to keep clean and her role was a very important one. Over the fifteen years I spent at St Luke's other personnel came and went but Lydia and I remained working together. Every Thursday from 10.15 to 11.45 am the ward was handed over to the domestic staff for the 'big clean' which made the twenty-bed section virtually a 'no-go' area. Beds, lockers and bed tables were pulled into the middle and the floor was scrubbed and dried before they were all cleaned and pushed back – first one side of the ward and then the other. Then the middle was very thoroughly done. The old beds were heavy to move and, like supermarket trolleys, had a mind of their own. Transfers were practically impossible, tempers frayed and all in all Thursday was very popular to have as a day off!

I could see at once that what St Catherine's Ward lacked in modern facilities it made up for with its warm and friendly welcome so I fitted myself in with existing routines and got to know the staff before making any adjustments. In addition to the midwives there was a team of part-time Nursing Auxiliaries and a Ward Receptionist called Eileen who worked 9am to 4.30 weekdays and soon became my right-hand woman. It was Eileen who provided my coffee and biscuits at 10.30 each morning, tapping my shoulder or waving to indicate that she had put them on my desk. She was a highly organised, methodical person – ideal characteristics for the job – and I was very sad when she left a few years later, especially as her replacement was a young girl straight from school with no midwifery background. I needn't have worried; Carolyn was excellent and remained on the staff for many years. I had the privilege of attending her wedding and eventually advised her to leave and get some qualifications, as she was clearly capable. My third receptionist, Pauline, bred spaniels so she was running her own, doggie Postnatal Ward at home! She was another great asset to St Cath's, keeping everything, including me, scrupulously up to date.

The first new baby I remember was a girl named Rebecca, born on May 23rd, to a Christian couple named Rosalind and Michael. They were a little younger than me and I got to know them quite well, as Rosalind had to be readmitted for further treatment and they, like me, were new to the area. They often invited me to tea, when I got to bath Becca, and when baby Vicky came along two years later I was asked to be her Godmother. A third daughter, Philippa followed five years later and I have remained a friend of the family, sharing important occasions with them.

During my first weeks I noticed a piece of slate on the shelf outside the office. It appeared to have no purpose and I was about to get rid of it when another midwife stopped me. "Just wait until there is a Consultant's round," she told me, "then you will see what it's used for!" The first time a Consultant and his retinue arrived in the ward I watched with interest as he took the lit cigarette out of his mouth, laid it carefully on the slate and left it burning there while he did his round. All became clear and the vital piece of slate stayed where it was!

There were three Consultants, two older – one a smoker – and one younger. All the patients' notes were colour-coded red, blue or green, according to which Consultant was in charge of that mum's care, and when one of them visited the appropriate notes were ready on a trolley to be pushed round so that he could have a word with those who were 'his'. As we returned to the office the older Consultant would pick up his cigarette and depart in a cloud of smoke. Fortunately, not long after I arrived, the two older Consultants retired, saving us from becoming smoked herrings!

Outside the office on the landing was a row of five chairs where people waited for visiting time. One afternoon I was doing some paperwork and having a cup of tea when I looked out and saw a little lad of about three or four sitting there alone, swinging his legs and reciting Humpty Dumpty to himself. I went out to investigate and he explained: "I'm a bit of a handful so Granny told me to come out here and say some nursery rhymes!" He then continued with Ba Ba Black Sheep. We had many older siblings brought to meet the new baby of the family by their grandmothers. Another one told me that, rushing to get out, she had asked: "William, do you want a wee?" and received the polite reply: "No, Thank you, Grandma, I make my own!"

A few years later while doing relief work in the community I visited a family with a little boy of a similar age, where I was offered coffee, which I accepted, and a butterfly cake, which I declined. The little boy had just had juice and a cake but wanted another one but his dad told him, "Not on your life!" At which the lad held up his plate and said "No, not on my life, on my plate!"

My first Christmas at Guildford saw a Beatrix Potter theme to the ward decorations. We made Plaster of Paris models of the characters and painted them to create a scene on the shelf outside the office, and my nativity stable was taken out of its black plastic sack and dusted off. That first year I made the mistake of putting baby Jesus in the manger a few days early, only to be told by an eight-year old visitor that He wasn't meant to be born until Christmas morning! In future years I gave Him to the night staff to be put in position at midnight on December 25th.

The hospital gave us £15 to cover ward Christmas expenses and we had to provide anything up to twenty baby stockings and gifts for mums. My own Mum and many others began knitting mittens, bootees and bonnets in September to ensure a plentiful supply. One of the Auxiliaries knitted toy dolls and another made animals; all the baby things were wrapped and put into cut-off tights for stockings. St Luke's didn't have a special cot for the first baby born on Christmas Day, so Eileen made one out of net curtaining and lace with a frilly hood fitted to a sturdy frame. Initially there were detachable blue or pink ribbons but later we made them in unisex lemon.

There was already a set routine for Christmas Day but I introduced the custom of sitting around the Christmas tree for a short carol service when we came on duty and before starting the morning's work. Sometimes a member of staff played guitar and on one occasion a new mum played, the guitar held at arm's length to accommodate her bump, which hadn't had time to reduce in size. Everyone seemed to enjoy this time, though it would not be permitted in these politically correct times. The only complaint we ever had was from a mum just returned from Theatre following a Caesarean. She was just about awake but very drowsy and when she heard *Hark the Herald Angels Sing* she thought she had died and was in heaven being welcomed by the angels!

After the carols we got the routine work done early so that the ward was ready for the visit from the Guildford Mayor. He would arrive resplendent in his chain of office and process around the ward with his entourage, congratulating everyone and having his photo taken with the first Christmas Day mum and baby. His PA and the Hospital Administrators who escorted him all did their best to keep him moving so that they could get home to their turkeys!

Meanwhile Father Christmas – one of the Registrars or Housemen – would be waiting patiently in the Obs and Gynae Theatre for the mayor to depart and the fathers and older siblings to arrive. The previous night, the second theatre trolley would have been transformed into Santa's sleigh, draped in green theatre towels and with a stool somewhat precariously balanced on it for Santa to sit on. This would be pushed into the ward by two Theatre Technicians dressed as elves in green scrubs, white boots and woolly hats. Fortunately Santa had the trolley rails to hold onto! Once in the ward he would produce gifts for all from a hessian sack. One year there were no male doctors on duty and we had to have a Mother Christmas, who said the sleigh ride part was terrifying! It was a lot of fun despite – or maybe because of – being a potential health and safety disaster.

Next the Salvation Army Band would play carols in the entrance hall and the uniformed ladies would come onto the ward to hand out more gifts, often including the staff. They would be closely followed by the lunch trolley at 12 o'clock complete with one enormous turkey big enough to feed all the mums and staff – up to thirty people. It was customary in hospitals for a Consultant to come in with their family to carve the turkey and for the fifteen years I was there we had the Driscolls. That first year the children were very young but still enjoyed helping. On one occasion their son was keen to set light to the pudding so I went to the medicine cupboard to fetch a bottle of 'medicinal' brandy. It must have been truly awful brandy because we hardly got a flicker of a flame! In the following years the Driscolls brought their own to much better effect. The youngsters really enjoyed carrying the lit pudding around the ward with everyone clapping.

One Festive season I remember a mum on the Antenatal Ward suddenly collapsing – a major abdominal blood vessel had ruptured, threatening her life. At any other time the outcome might have been very different but Mr Coates, a Consultant Obstetrician was there on turkey-carving duty and Santa's helpers, the Theatre staff, were immediately available as well. It was a near thing but mother and baby survived the experience. When they arrived on St Catherine's Ward some time later, the mum told us how she'd had an 'out of body experience' while staff fought for her life.

Another year Lydia's mother and nephew spent Christmas Day on the ward helping her with her work and joining the staff for lunch. In my early days at St Like's the staff ate on the ward after the mums had been fed. Soon after lunch a second food delivery came from the kitchen as a buffet for supper. The ward fridge was quite small so I rigged up a 'cold room' on the balcony having first double wrapped everything, covered it in tea towels and done my best to make the area pigeon-proof! During afternoon tea Christmas cake was served to everyone – how I remember those cakes with their concrete-like icing, and what a job it was to cut them!

Our efforts did not go unappreciated. I still have a cutting from the letters page of the local newspaper, where one of our patients was moved to reply to a derogatory article about Christmas at St Luke's that had been published the week before. *"I spent Christmas in St Catherine's Ward at St Luke's and have nothing but admiration for the catering staff,"* she wrote. *"We did have an intact turkey, carved by Mr Driscoll, Consultant Gynaecologist, and served to us by his wife and children, plus all the trimmings and fresh vegetables followed by a choice of two desserts. It was all beautifully cooked and nicely served by the nursing staff..." "...I gather that the staff on St Catherine's Ward started to prepare for Christmas in the middle of last summer. They had made many beautiful decorations which were put up around the ward on December 21st*

*and had knitted and crocheted many small
gifts for our newborn babies. The staff who had
to work over the holiday were extremely
cheerful and made our day as near as possible
to a family Christmas. I would not have said
they had 'lost heart' – rather the reverse. Your
article must worry anyone who might have to
spend Christmas in hospital, but both patients
and visitors at St Catherine's Ward had a very
happy time and I would like to take this
opportunity to thank everyone who helped
make it so."*

It was very gratifying to be on the receiving
end of such public praise, but had I been
inclined to let it go to my head and become too
self-important, ward life would soon have
cured me. One memorable Christmas
afternoon I was chatting with a family and the
child was showing me his toy cars and
demonstrating how fast they went. Of course
one ended up stuck under the bed-head on
the side where I was standing so I knelt down
to try to retrieve it and found it out of my
reach. There was nothing for it but to crawl
under the bed. It was then that I heard quite a
posh male voice enquiring, "Do you know
where I might find the Ward Sister?" To which
the father of the family replied, "She's on the
floor under the bed!" I reversed out, stood up
with my cap askew and, mustering as much

dignity as I could manage, said "May I help you?" The visitor must have thought he had wandered onto the set of a Carry-On film!

Soon after I had completed my first year at St Luke's I was told I would have to move out of the Nurses Home flat and was offered accommodation in the attics of a Geriatric Hospital in the nearby village of Puttenham. I went to visit it one afternoon and found that a strong smell of urine pervaded the entire building. I thought if I lived there all my clothes would soon smell the same so I began to look elsewhere and a colleague said she had heard of someone in another local village, Albury, who wanted a lodger. This turned out to be a wonderful family whose home I shared for the next eighteen months. However I was still keen to get on the property ladder and I continued to save for a deposit on a flat of my own.

The route to and from work was along very narrow country lanes, most of them single-track with passing places. One summer evening I was making my way home around 8.45pm when I saw a large white van speeding towards me. I pulled over opposite the driveway of a large house to give it room to get past me but it continued to hurtle straight at me and I knew it was going to hit me, which it did. I got out and so did the van driver, an unpleasant man who started shouting at me and was soon joined by his passenger. I felt very intimidated and went up the driveway of the house to ring the doorbell and ask for help. As soon as the owner came out – a businessman just back from London – white-van-man immediately changed his attitude and I was allowed to move my car into the driveway while details were exchanged and formalities completed. Once the van had gone my rescuer insisted I sit down and have a brandy, which may not have been such a good idea since I had not eaten since midday!

That October, Guildford became the centre of attention when IRA bombs exploded at the Horse and Groom and Seven Stars pubs killing five people and injuring many more. Both pubs were used by Army personnel and many of the casualties were soldiers recently returned from tours of duty in Northern Ireland. Within hours the hospital had drawn up procedures to be followed should either St Luke's or the Royal Surrey Hospital receive a telephoned bomb threat. Along with all the others, the Maternity Department had to practise evacuation drills, roping patients to mattresses in order to move them downstairs.

On a lighter note, a month later Britain's first MacDonald's opened in Woolwich, number 3000 in the World. Forty years later there are more than 30 000 branches, 1200 of them in the UK and the brand, along with others like Coca cola and David Beckham, is recognised all around what is a very different world.

In the summer of 1975 I had to go on another residential refresher course. This time I chose to go to Leeds – I had friends living and working there so it was an opportunity to visit them, especially Margaret who I had met back at the Masonic Hospital and who had introduced me to the Nurses Christian Fellowship. The day before I went I took delivery of a new car and was driving it up the M1when the windscreen suddenly shattered. Looking to pull over I realised I was just approaching the slip-road to a service station where I found a repair man to replace the windscreen and was on my way again very quickly. Someone was looking after me that day!

Chapter Eleven

After three years of saving, eighteen months lodging in Albury and interminable legal manoeuvring by solicitors, I finally took possession of my own home in Bisley not long before the Christmas of 1975. It was a bitterly cold and wet day when my Dad and Uncle loaded all my gear into a van and drove it to Surrey: meanwhile I was still in Albury, waiting for the AA to come and sort out the electrics on my car as I had no lights or windscreen wipers! The heating in my new flat was night storage; it had been turned off for two days and that first night was so cold that, despite multiple layers of blankets and an old eiderdown, I lay awake shivering until morning. After that inauspicious start, I settled in well.

This was my first winter of driving to and from Guilford in the snow and ice, and soon I got into the routine of taking a small bag of essentials with me to enable an overnight stay in the Nurses Home if necessary. The boot of my car always contained an old electric sewing machine to weigh the back-end down and a shovel to clear a path out of the car park! Warren Road, which led to St Lukes, was a very difficult prospect when covered in black ice.

Surrey residents of the late seventies onwards became very familiar with Concorde, the beautiful but very noisy airplane which began commercial flights out of Heathrow in January 1976. People would stop what they were doing to watch her – indeed it was impossible to continue a conversation or concentrate on doing anything else for the brief time the aircraft was overhead. It was the dream of many people to someday fly on one. I never managed that, although I did set foot on one at Brooklands Museum after they had all been taken out of service and even that was exciting.

During that spring I was sent for a while as a relief Midwifery Sister to St George's Wood Maternity Unit in Hazlemere while theirs was recovering from surgery. Although I enjoyed being back on a Labour Ward, the fact that I lived half an hour's drive away unfortunately meant that I had to sleep there when on call. It took me a while to get used to the new routine and to Cottage Hospital ways. Later that year St George's Wood closed and the Maternity Unit moved to Princess Margaret Rose Ward in Hazlemere Hospital – officially opened by Princess Margaret. Nine years later that too closed and everyone, including some of the staff members, had to come to St Luke's; it was a very difficult time for all concerned.

There was a sizeable Dutch community in the Guildford area and they had a tradition of celebrating on the second or third day after a birth with little cakes or biscuits sprinkled with pink or blue liquorice. This was a wonderful encouragement to the bowels, especially after difficult forceps deliveries – much preferable to laxatives! Another cure from abroad was introduced by an Aussie Registrar who advocated runny honey for perineums that were slow to heal. Manuka honey was considered the best and is now the most expensive, but back in the fifties Kiwi farmers fed it to their cattle to boost nourishment during the winter.

Although midwifery practice was being modernised all the time, some old remedies were still in common use. Uncooked cabbage leaves were laid inside nursing bras to relieve painful engorged breasts; lightly whisked egg white was applied to babies' sore bottoms, making sure that it dried completely and didn't stick; a strong-smelling tar compound called glycerine of ichthyol (known as *glyc and Ic*) would be applied to inflamed veins; and tincture of benzoin (*tinc benz*) to a cracked nipple.

The twice-daily salt bath for mothers was sacrosanct but not always properly understood by the patients. I remember examining a mum on her fourth day and finding her perineum inexplicably red raw and bleeding. Accompanying her to the bathroom I was horrified to find she was rubbing handfuls of salt into herself rather than diluting it in the water! I had to explain to her that 'more' is not necessarily 'better'. When helping another mum with her first postnatal bath I said I would leave her for a few minutes to enjoy her soak and she was genuinely terrified. "Oh Sister, please don't leave me," she begged, tears in her eyes, "I can't swim!" I had visions of installing red and white life belts in all the bathrooms.

Phobias about blood and needles were very common. I remember one mum who passed out at the very mention of the word 'blood'. Another husband refused to visit just in case he had to pass the bed of someone having a transfusion. Breastfeeding was increasing in popularity and I spent a lot of time helping mums to do this successfully, for which they were very grateful. I remember one day on a visit to Hampton Court Palace I was sitting on a bench near the maze when a family passed by and the mother said to me, "You're Sister Roberts! Do you remember helping me years ago to breast feed?" Another time I was walking on the Malvern Hills and had the same conversation with a young couple coming in the opposite direction with a baby in a sling.

Obstetric experience was included in the syllabus of student nurses and a big part of my job was teaching them, along with the pupil midwives. I enjoyed watching out for the gifted ones who I knew would go further in their careers than me. Some of the students had such quiet voices that the mums had trouble hearing what they said when demonstrating baby baths or explaining how to make up bottle feeds. To try to get them to project their voices I would take them into an empty nursery and get them to speak to me at greater and greater distances. Their mother-craft classes improved greatly once they could actually be heard.

One of the GPs who came into the hospital asked if I would be prepared to have a young girl come in on a Saturday morning to help out on the ward. He had been working with the family and knew she loved babies and had a lot of younger siblings but no confidence. When he brought her to meet me she was painfully shy but, over the next two years I saw her come out of her shell and learn how to interact normally with other people. I often wonder how life turned out for her.

My friend, Mary had been working in Ethiopia but in May of 1977 like most British workers she was hurriedly flown home due to escalating unrest in the country. She took a temporary midwifery post at St Luke's and lived with me in Bisley while she decided what to do next. By then I had managed to wean myself completely from antidepressants – it had been very difficult but by gradually decreasing the dose I had finally done it – so both of us could appreciate the celebratory feel in the air as the country geared itself up for the Queen's Silver Jubilee celebrations in the summer. On the day itself, St Cath's staff and patients gathered in the Day Room to watch the procession and service in St Paul's cathedral and we had a special menu that included Jubilee Soup. This was a basic chicken soup (white) with tomato or pepper (red) and pieces of either quorn or tofu coloured blue – it was certainly colourful and patriotic but I don't remember it being a great success gastronomically!

The celebrations continued nationwide and I took two friends home to the Isle of Wight to enjoy the Review of the Fleet in the Solent. Britain had many warships in those days and it was very impressive to see them all lined up, especially when they were 'dressed overall', Dressing a ship overall with bunting is only done in harbour to celebrate special occasions like regattas, national festivals and the

Queen's birthday, and the Admiralty lays down a carefully arranged sequence of flags for all to follow, starting from the bow to the stern via the mast head, and guaranteed not to signal any offensive words in any language!

At night I drove my father's car onto Ashey Down for a good view of the fireworks and to see the enormous aircraft carriers floodlit. To get a close-up view in daylight we later took a trip on a car ferry from Fishbourne to Portsmouth and then back again. It was a beautiful sunny afternoon and the ferry carefully made its way along the lanes between the fleet. I remember there was a great sense of occasion on the island with many people holding beach picnics. With Virginia Wade becoming Wimbledon champion that summer it was a time of great national pride remembered fondly for many years to come.

*

Ward teams were in a constant state of flux, as trained staff rotated around all the Midwifery Departments. The only static personnel on the postnatal floor were the Auxiliaries, the Ward Receptionist and me! By this time a number of pupil midwives from my early days at Guildford had finished training, become Staff Midwives and been promoted to

Midwifery Sisters themselves. The first I remember was a girl named Barbara who became Second Sister on St Catherine's Ward and eventually married an Australian Obstetric Registrar called Ralph. Very soon after this we had a second wedding to celebrate when a Sister called Sally married Ken, the Obstetric Houseman who was also an Australian – there must have been something about those antipodeans! Both couples subsequently moved to Australia to live and work.

From time to time I did some relief Community Midwifery, mainly at the weekends. This was the first time I had worked 'on the district' since my pupil midwife days in Sholing but I soon got to know all the back lanes and short cuts of Surrey. Some addresses did present a bit of a challenge, like *Two Trees, Forest Road* – Forest Road was about a mile long and the name 'Two Trees' could have applied to most of its houses! At one home I visited the family had only moved in the previous day and not all of the sinks or baths had been connected to the water supply. I ended up bathing the baby in the brand-new bidet!

Although the area was known as the 'stockbroker belt' there was still a lot of poverty in the area. Some of the poorer houses around the Guildford station were due to be demolished to make way for flats and businesses – I remember one where the people had been desperate enough to pull up the front room floorboards and use them for firewood the previous winter. In the seventies it was not uncommon to find the bath behind a curtain in the kitchen. I visited one family who stored loose coal in such a bath and the husband had to shovel it out and clean the bath before it could be used for its intended purpose.

At another house I went to collect a towel from the airing cupboard and found a pile of four familiar-looking cot blankets with *St Luke's Hospital* printed on them. I said I'd found the blankets they had 'borrowed' to keep the baby warm when bringing it home and offered to return them and save the family a journey. Grandma looked very embarrassed! So much of our baby linen went missing in this way; we were always ringing the laundry, desperate for nappies and blankets, especially at weekends.

The very long labours some mums had to endure in those days could trigger mental conditions known as puerperal psychoses. People having psychiatric meltdowns in the middle of a large ward were never easy to handle and it was always a relief when they were transferred. I remember one woman whose behaviour was quite bizarre and out of touch with reality; I looked after her while we waited for her to be transferred to Brookwood, our local Psychiatric Hospital. Some years later I found myself visiting her at home following the birth of her second baby and was surprised when she said, "Thank you for being so kind to me when I was having my attacks last time." I had not expected her to remember anything about it. It was a big lesson to me not to make assumptions about those with mental health problems.

Several of the local clergy would come into the ward to visit members of their fellowships – I found most of them caring and helpful, especially when people were having problems. Another regular visitor to St Cath's was the Registrar of Births and Deaths, who would arrive just after lunch, four days a week. Although people had six weeks in which to get their baby registered, it was very helpful for them to be able to do it before they went home, and saved them a trip to the Registry Office.

1978 was a very exciting year for Obstetrics, as Louise Brown, the first test-tube baby, was born in July in Oldham. It was to be several more years before an IVF baby was born at St Luke's and the event was shrouded in secrecy – even though the science of IVF had progressed rapidly in the meantime it was still considered controversial by some people. Only a few midwives were in on the secret, the parents being unsure how it would be received.

Since I arrived in Surrey I had been attending Holy Trinity Church in the nearby village of Knaphill and become a member the previous year. That August I went with several others to The Dales Bible Week at the Great North Showground in Harrogate. It meant camping – something I had only done once before at the Keswick Convention, another Christian event in the Lake District. On that occasion the weather had been awful and it had not been a great success, so I was looking forward to this with distinctly mixed feelings! Three teenage girls piled into my Fiat for the drive north. Most of their luggage had to go in other vehicles but they were all packed around with pillows and sleeping bags.

The weather could not have been worse and the whole experience could have been at unmitigated disaster, but I remember it as a wonderful Spiritual experience and the time when many lasting friendships were forged. The Boxall, Clarke, Hayhoe and Chowney families all became lifelong and very special friends and over the next ten years I attended various school functions, took Kate and

Graham Boxall and Graeme and Simon Clarke on outings, often to the Isle of Wight. I feel very honoured to have been part of these families and to be included in their sadnesses as well as their joys.

While I worked at St Luke's I attended a number of further-education courses, often going to London on day-release over a period of three months. One was at the Tavistock Clinic, at the time an important Psychiatric Clinic in terms of training as well as treatment. It was a nightmare to get to, especially getting across the city during the rush-hour. Another course I went on was at the Wolfenden Rehabilitation Centre in Wimbledon and this one was a lot easier to access by car up the A3. Both these courses were linked to bereavement – this was a time when better care for families who had suffered a miscarriage or still-birth was becoming a much higher priority. Following on from these I also did a listener's counselling course, which was very useful both in midwifery and in my future role as Parish Worker at Holy Trinity Church.

Twice a year I spent a day in London at the headquarters of the Royal College of Midwives, which was situated near the BBC at the top of Regents Street. Two representatives of the Guildford Branch of the RCM – one from the hospital and one from the community – went to the meetings to hear the latest news and then report back to the local members. It was a good time to meet up with friends and enjoy browsing along Oxford Street! All Maternity Units were inspected by the Central Midwives Board, in much the same way as schools have OFSTED inspections today and these, while necessary, were always very stressful.

Change over which we have no control is another major cause of stress, and for several years the midwifery management structure had been in a constant state of remodelling – first the addition of an extra tier and then the merging of the roles of Nursing Officer and Senior Nursing Officer, while the Superintendent became the Divisional Nursing Officer. Now plans were afoot to combine the Maternity Units at St Peter's Hospital Chertsey, Frimley Park Hospital and St Luke's into one Midwifery School. It was thought that this would save a lot of money. The tutorial staff would merge and move around the three sites; some tutorials would be done in the clinical areas by the Midwifery Tutors but trained ward staff would undertake much of the practical instruction.

An enjoyable and absorbing task can be a great antidote to stress. One of the jobs I enjoyed doing was working out the weekly ward rotas – this was my crossword puzzle and it was sometimes quite a headache trying to fulfil everyone's requests! Another responsibility I had was the employment of Nursing Auxiliaries. They did tend to stay in post quite a long time but when a vacancy arose it was my responsibility to interview and recruit a replacement. I recall one young girl who came hoping for a day post and, as always, I asked her to fill out a form in front of me so I could be sure that she knew how to read and write. Everything seemed in order and she was offered the job. Each baby's cot had a chart where details of feeding and output were recorded along with the date and time, and I could not understand why the new Auxiliary never seemed to complete these forms properly. When I had a chat with her about it I found out that she had never learnt to tell the time.

Other staff members were apparently finding themselves with time on their hands. Around this time it was noticed that the phones on St Catherine's Ward were making an excessive number of calls at night to overseas numbers. A cap was soon put in place that restricted these calls and prevented staff from spending quiet nights contacting far-flung family at the hospital's expense!

Chapter Twelve

Towards the end of 1979 I asked my boss if I could have leave of absence because I wanted to go to Israel for three months as a volunteer with the CMJ (Church's Ministry among Jewish people). I had three weeks holiday owing to me and she gave me a further two-and-a-half months of unpaid leave, keeping my job open for me, so this gave me thirteen weeks in all. I left the UK early the following April on the Israeli airline El-Al (back then it was said to stand for *'Every Landing Always Late'*, though it has a far better reputation now!). It took five hours to fly to Tel Aviv and, as the plane touched down, all the Jewish passengers began to clap and sing Hebrew songs. Many of them knelt to kiss the ground as they disembarked – an expression of their joy at being in Israel and not of lack of confidence in El Al!

Bridget the CMJ representative was in the Arrivals Hall to greet me and together we drove to Stella Carmel, a conference and retreat centre on Mount Carmel above Haifa. It was on the outskirts of Isfiyah, a place that I would come to know and love. A Druse village, it looked down into the Jezreel Valley – at dusk transformed into a fairyland of twinkling lights from the Arab villages and the Kibbutz. Here I was welcomed into the Stella Carmel family and very quickly got to know people. There were eight volunteers – six women and two men – and we all lived, worked and spent our leisure time together. In addition to a little pocket money we each received two airmail letters per fortnight to send home. In those days before email and mobile phones, and with payphones being very expensive, this was our only way of keeping in touch with friends and family. Our mail, like our stores, had to be fetched by car from Haifa. Everyone was always keen to see if there was a letter for them and, if there was, would slip away somewhere quiet to read it in peace.

The six female volunteers shared three twin-bedded rooms in a bungalow. We also shared a bathroom, toilet, laundry and kitchenette, which was where we gathered to listen to a selection of 78s played on an old record player. Our favourite, *Bridge over Troubled Water* by Simon and Garfunkel, could be heard morning, noon and night on a daily basis! There was a TV in the Managers' flat but the only time I recall us watching it was, rather sadly, for the Eurovision Song Contest! One evening, while walking through the village past a bar, a group of us heard the unmistakeable sound of tennis being played and realised it was a recording of a Wimbledon match so we went inside to watch. The sounds on the radio of Big Ben chiming and the BBC pips were also nostalgic reminders of a home that seemed very far away.

Every morning, except on our day off, we began the day with prayers in the Chapel before breakfast. Each of us took it in turn to lead the fifteen-minute devotion and this could feel rather intimidating if all the CMJ Israel clergy were in attendance – a bit like having to preach a sermon to the Archbishop of Canterbury! The daily work was mainly domestic; physically hard but much less stressful than midwifery – we had one day off a week and a monthly long weekend. All of the Christian Retreat Centres in Israel had a reciprocal policy of hosting each other's volunteers for a nominal amount and it was usually arranged for two or three of us to go off together for our three-night breaks. I enjoyed two such weekends – one in Jerusalem and the other in Tiberius by the Sea of Galilee where the Church of Scotland had a wonderful centre that had previously been a hospital and is now a four-star hotel in private hands.

Travel on the local buses could be slow but it was always full of interest. I recall sharing the back of a bus with a sheep and its owner and also several infinitely smaller creatures whose presence only became evident when I began to itch that evening. Another interesting bus-ride incorporated an unscheduled stop so that the driver could deliver a package to his family and collect some furniture to take into Nazareth. The cupboard was wedged into the gangway between the seats.

There was no washing machine at the bungalow – all our washing was done in an old sink, wrung out as well as we could and hung on the line inside-out so that the outside did not fade in the strong sunlight. On one occasion we came back from lunch in the main house to find four T-shirts missing from the line – it seemed some local youths had used a rubbish tip to climb over the back wall and taken them. Two of them were mine, one a very distinctive rust-coloured one with check collar and cuffs. A week later, walking in the woods on Mount Carmel, we came across a group of youths, one of them wearing my T-shirt. It was annoying to see him flaunting what he'd stolen from me, but there was nothing we could do about it. While the villagers were usually friendly we were not encouraged to wander about alone.

What we did have was an abundance of wildlife, indoors and out. Cockroaches, scorpions and spiders were common and we were even visited by the occasional snake. I remember the day one was spotted disappearing behind the filing cabinets in the office; it was generally believed that snakes went around in pairs so an intensive search was made for the other one, with no success. (There does not appear to be any truth in this belief!)

Apart from the buses, another local form of transport was the sherut, or shared taxi. The aim of the driver was to pack as many people in as possible and make as many journeys per day as he could in order to maximise profit. At least twice when using this I seriously doubted I would get out in one piece and felt extremely relieved to do so! The trip from Isfiyah to Haifa, though only a few miles, was scary in the extreme for the seven or eight tightly-wedged passengers, as we careered at top speed down steep, narrow mountain roads and around hairpin bends.

On one terrifying occasion I was en-route to Ben Gurion Airport near Tel Aviv, belting along a dual carriageway that all the traffic seemed to treat as a race-track, when another sherut drew alongside and its driver reached across and held hands with the front-seat passenger in mine! A fleet of these vehicles shuttled tourists up the road to the top of Mount Tabor with its multiple-hair-pins, and the drivers delighted in frightening their passengers. The first time I went up by taxi, I decided it would be safer to walk back down, and got some very good photos by doing so! Afterwards we found out that each one of these vehicles, many of which looked ready to fall apart, had to have a regular safety overhaul by a Nazareth motor mechanic.

There were a number of occasions when my training came in useful, even though I was not at Stella in the official capacity of nurse. Once we were clearing the tables between lunch courses for a ninety-strong, mixed group of Lutheran Arab Christians who had come for a holiday retreat, when an elderly lady fell to the floor having convulsions. She was recovering from the removal of a brain tumour and I was able to take care of her until a doctor from the village arrived. The fit didn't last for long and the lady was fine, but it was rather frightening and dramatic for the other people there. Not one of them would eat their dessert, leaving us with ninety portions of unwanted melon that had to go in the bin! There is not a lot that can be done with watermelon, once cut up.

Another time an English couple arrived having come via the Dead Sea and Masada, where the man had fallen and grazed his knee. Three days later he was still hobbling, feeling very ill and running a temperature, and his knee was swollen and inflamed – infections were a common hazard following any sort of

abrasion incurred at Masada. After speaking
to the doctor on duty at the Haifa Hospital
Casualty Department the man was transferred
nine miles down the mountain and remained
in the hospital for several days having
intravenous antibiotics.

Alongside our gardening, cleaning and
waiting duties, we also did food preparation in
the kitchen. The cook was a lovely, caring,
motherly woman known to all as 'Auntie
Mary', an Arab Christian who had been
coming up from Haifa on a daily basis for
years. On a Saturday morning, however, it was
the volunteers who prepared lunch. I recall
being the middle one of three women chopping
vegetables for coleslaw when the girl to my left
cut her finger quite badly. She held it up for
us to see and the blood was dripping onto the
waste cabbage, whereupon the girl to my right
said "I think I'm going to faint!" With one hand
I grabbed a clean tea-towel, wrapped it around
the injured finger and held the arm up in the
air; with the other I pushed the fainting girl's
head down between her knees – it's a wonder
we didn't all fall off our stools! Order was
restored and lunch eventually served, albeit a
little late.

CMJ staff from elsewhere would sometimes
come to Stella for a quiet weekend or for
conferences. There was one time when all the

Jerusalem staff came at once with their families. We did our best to entertain the eight-to-ten-year-olds with games and treasure-hunts but they often had to keep themselves amused when we were busy. On the Saturday afternoon we prepared tea, the cake was iced and on the trolley, the small urn was coming to the boil in the hallway, and milk and sweeteners were put out ready for the CMJ officials to pour the tea for themselves. As they sipped from their cups, a look of disgust appeared on every face – the tea tasted awful! We later found out that two of the little boys had put handfuls of sweeteners and salt into the tea urn and then watched from a distance to enjoy the result!

Volunteers were not insured to drive the CMJ vehicles so outings depended on the abundant goodwill of the staff members. One quiet Sunday afternoon we were taken to swim at Atlit beach, which I much preferred to the beach at Haifa. It had been a very busy spell and this was a brief hiatus before the next influx of guests, so two carloads of us headed eagerly for the sands with our picnics. The sea was a bit rough that day but the lifeguards considered it safe to swim. As I was not a strong swimmer I was making sure that I did not go out of my depth, when a big wave knocked me over and the next one dragged me under the water and further out to sea. My friends shouted for help and I was carried, coughing and spluttering from the sea by a handsome lifeguard – an experience I was in no condition to appreciate! He dumped me unceremoniously on the sand in the recovery position, where it took me a few minutes to get over the shock, only to find that the younger girls were quite put out that my rescuer had been wasted on me!

Twice during my time as a volunteer I went down to the late-night cinema in Haifa. The first time I saw Kramer versus Kramer with Meryl Streep and Dustin Hoffman, which I very much enjoyed. The second time I sat through Apocalypse Now, the horrific Vietnamese war film starring Marlon Brando, though I can't really say that I 'saw' it as I spent a lot of time with my eyes firmly shut! The noise of the battle onscreen was intensified by the sound of drinks cans and bottles rolling down the uncarpeted, raked flooring of the cinema! Both films had been released the previous year but this was their first showing in Haifa – the spoken language was English but there were Hebrew and Arabic subtitles.

I spent ten weeks in all at Stella Carmel. When I arrived, the countryside was green and covered in spring flowers, and the white walls of the retreat showed off the pink and mauve bougainvillea flowers, which looked beautiful in the sunshine. Slowly the river beds dried up and the landscape grew dry and barren-looking, only enlivened by the splashes of pink and white provided by the oleander bushes. A rare and wonderful event was a view of Mount Hermon's snow-capped, 9230-foot peak – most of the time it was shrouded in cloud. Twice during my stay it became visible and everyone rushed out to the terrace to see it. Another much-recommended natural phenomenon was the sight of a blood-red moon. We got up at two in the morning to see this and most of us were distinctly unimpressed, feeling that the description 'blood red' was something of an exaggeration!

When my time as a volunteer came to an end Mary arrived to join me and we set off for a holiday, beginning at the Sea of Galilee and then making our way down to Jerusalem. I had booked some nights at Eilat, which was situated on the Red Sea coast, a five-hour bus ride from Jerusalem down the Jordan Valley. Unfortunately, an hour after departure the air conditioning failed and from then on the journey was an ordeal, as more and more people crammed onto the bus, most of them chain smoking, while the temperature outside rose to more than 40°. By the time we arrived at our destination we were exhausted, hot, smelly and not at all in a holiday mood.

In those days there was very little at Eilat – a bus station, a small airfield, a few hotels and some apartments up the hill from the beach, but what should have been enjoyable days on the beach were overshadowed by the thought of the return journey to Jerusalem. I did have a contingency fund – some extra travellers' cheques in case of an emergency – and I decided that this was that emergency! We flew back up the Jordan Valley, a wonderful forty-five minute trip in a small plane, during which we saw Bedouin tents and camel trains making their way across the Negev to Beersheeba. It might have been a bit bumpy but it was worth every penny.

Before we left I spent quite a bit of money on four Palestinian placemats, embroidered in a traditional cross-stitch design similar to that seen on the long, black garments worn by women in the Middle East. Someone had spent many hours stitching those placemats and I treasured them and still use them on special occasions. I remember as the plane circled over Heathrow preparing to land, looking down and being struck by the greenness of the late-July countryside below.

As soon as I arrived home I had to arrange a refresher course. Because I had been away I was very late in booking it and had little choice as to where I would go, but places were available in Birmingham so I duly booked myself onto that one. It was not too inconvenient, as I had friends in the area with whom I had an enjoyable stay for the weekend beforehand, but finding my way through the city centre on the first day of the course was quite confusing – I must have passed the Bull Ring three times! This was the year of the Rubik's Cube when the craze was at its height and it was as common to see people walking around with them as it is to see people with mobile phones today.

The course was held in the university complex near the old Cadbury buildings, and it would be my third. I could hardly believe that I had now been employed in hospitals for twenty years! While there I met a Southampton pupil of mine who was on her second refresher course; it was always a pleasure to meet up with ex colleagues and catch up with their news.

That autumn at the Royal College of Midwives meeting the talk was all about plans for celebrating its centenary the following year. Designs had been submitted for celebratory tea-towels and plates and a nursery had been commissioned to breed a new rose for the occasion – a climbing apricot flowered variety. The competition to name the rose was won by *Breath of Life* and it is still available in garden centres now. A gardening website says, *"The name was chosen by Britain's Royal College of Midwives to signify the Creator spirit in Genesis and also the first thing everyone must do after being born into the world."*

It was in the early eighties that I began to see the first cases of babies born with alcohol dependence – they were a pitiful sight in the incubators, so tiny and having 'the shakes', and they were comforted through the first days of their lives with phenobarbitone and cuddles. Around this time a number of changes were being made on St Catherine's Ward; two beds were taken out of the large ward to enable babies to stay with their mothers during the day and visiting time was increased. Now the mothers had a lot more bonding time with their babies and could have two or three visitors every afternoon between three and four, but only their husband or partner between seven and eight in the evening.

One set of grandparents were very concerned to learn that the baby had slightly webbed toes. Trying to be reassuring I said to the grandfather that I was sure there would be others in the family with the same condition, but he was astounded at the suggestion, he had never heard of such a thing! A couple of evenings later the baby's father stopped by the office to tell me that all the family had been instructed to inspect their feet and, to the grandfather's amazement, many of them, including himself, had some degree of webbing between their toes!

The new mums came to us on trolleys complete with their belongings, flowers and babies. By the eighties they were being encouraged to move around and bathe much sooner after the birth, doing away with most of the swabbing. Every morning each mum and baby was examined to make sure both were progressing well. Disposable nappies were now becoming more widely-used and were still provided by the National Health Service. They did cut down on washing and were easier to put on, provided the adhesive patches were not touched by fingers that had just applied Vaseline. I campaigned for years to persuade Pampers to produce disposables for the newborn with crescent shaped cut-outs at the front so that the cord was left uncovered. Without that it was very difficult to keep cords dry and we seemed to get a lot of 'sticky' cords with low-grade infections requiring extra cleaning and Sterzac. Huggies launched such a nappy nearly thirty years later in August 2011, but as far as I know Pampers has yet to do so.

Another minor infection suffered by some babies was 'sticky eyes' requiring intensive use of chloramphenicol eye drops, gradually decreasing in frequency, and the application of these was done by a midwife wearing a white protective gown to avoid cross-infection by contaminated uniform. This was a very popular job as it meant sitting down and cuddling the baby! Neonatal care was improving all the time and continues to do so. In 1900 out of every 1000 babies born, 160 died before their first birthday – in the 1981 census the mortality figure had dropped to eleven. One in eight required time in SCBU and only 20 percent of babies born weighing less than 2lb 2oz survived to thrive. With all the technology available today, that figure continues to rise and at the time of writing is nearing fifty percent.

St Catherine's Ward got out the bunting and union flags again for the wedding of Prince Charles to Lady Diana Spencer in July. The ceremony in St Paul's Cathedral was televised and most of the staff and mums watched – part of an estimated global audience of 750 million. I remember around that time a lot of stories on the news about the problems of chemotherapy and how it reduced the patient's antibodies making them more susceptible to infections. In the grounds of St Luke's we had the Guildford Oncology Centre, one of the leading Cancer Treatment Units in the UK.

One evening I was preparing to give the night staff the 8pm report when a young woman rushed up the stairs in tears. She had a young baby which she had stopped breastfeeding six weeks before. Now her husband was here having treatment for cancer and his antibodies had dropped to nearly zero. She remembered being encouraged to breastfeed because it provided antibodies for the baby and she wanted to use the electric breast pump so that she could express breast-milk for her husband to have in his coffee. It was an unusual request but it was something she could do for him. The stimulation of the pump produced a good flow and enough milk to make drinks for several nights. Unfortunately the man died soon after, but it was worth a try.

Whenever possible the hospital tried to accommodate patients' wishes, even when they were out of the ordinary. A long-stay mum-to-be was missing her favourite horse, so he was brought to the car park in a horsebox, unloaded and taken to the window

of the Antenatal Ward (outside, not inside!).
She was very happy to see him, unlike the
porters who had to come round afterwards
with a shovel. They were called in for more
zoological duties when the pigeons found out
how to get into the changing room, which was
up two flights of stairs in the attic. I once
found one on top of a locker sitting on two
eggs, having nested there and, another time,
encountered one walking around on a toilet
having messed on the seat! The squatters were
evacuated and wire was fitted over the
windows.

In the middle of the night early in 1982 I
was woken by the sound of army transporters,
lorries and equipment trundling past my flat
on their way from nearby Pirbright Camp
down to the south coast to embark for the
Falkland Islands, which had been invaded by
the Argentineans. I sat up and watched them
out of my window, hoping that all the soldiers
would return safely. More than a hundred
ships made their way down the Atlantic where
the conflict went on from the end of April until
mid June, when General Menendez
surrendered. By then 255 British lives had
been lost, along with 649 Argentineans.

Days and weeks went by with nothing
happening outside of the normal routine but
we always had to be prepared for an

emergency. Every ward had an adult resuscitation trolley which was checked every day by a Theatre Technician to ensure it was ready for use should we have a cardiac arrest. If there was a problem with a baby requiring more attention than we could provide, it was quickly transferred to SCBU.

I recall one occasion when I was very pleased that the resuscitation trolley was ready for use with everything in working order. The mum occupying the bed in the most inconvenient spot in the ward suddenly collapsed and we had very little space to work in, as there was a wall on one side of her and a doorway on the other. She was transferred to the Royal Surrey and a midwife went and did a post-natal visit every morning until she was returned to us a few days later. On another occasion I was walking past a bed in which a patient, recovering from her third Caesarean and not in good health, could be heard coughing. All at once there was a shriek and she called out to me, "Sister, something's happened!" Indeed something had – her stitches had burst and she was returned to Theatre to be re-sutured. Even in the days before neat, bikini-line incisions this was rare.

Something that happened every Saturday was the antenatal visit by *primips* and their partners – usually enjoyable but sometimes a bit fraught on busy weekends. Each time I would explain the same things, trying to make it interesting. We encouraged the women to bring old or preferably disposable knickers so I would say, "The best disposable pants are in Boots; look on the shelf below the ladies' ones and you will find the men's – far roomier and much more comfortable!" The men would look sideways at each other and we would have a laugh trying to guess which of them might wear disposable pants.

In the autumn of 1984 once again it was 'all-change' for the maternity management teams. My boss encouraged me to apply for the Clinical Nurse Specialist post covering the Postnatal Ward and SCBU. I was interviewed by two Obstetricians, the Divisional Nursing Officer and the Senior Midwifery Tutor and was fortunate enough to be offered the place, taking up my new post on the first of December 1984.

Chapter Thirteen

It felt a little strange to be wearing a different
uniform and cap as I climbed the stairs to the
Midwifery Office floor. The old Board Room
still existed alongside the offices of the
Divisional Officer and her PA. The Midwifery
Secretaries had an office, as did the three
general Clinical Nurse Specialists and the
Community Senior Midwife. Most importantly
there was a small kitchen essential for making
coffee. Promoted at the same time as me was
Lesley, who was now CNS for the Labour and
Gynae Wards. Usually we worked opposite
weekends, each covering for the other's
'patch'. We both soon settled into our roles
and I still enjoyed the teaching part of the job.

The offices of the CNSs on the general side
were moving over to the Royal Surrey Hospital
in the near future, still in Guildford but near
the Cathedral and University. Although the
Maternity Unit would not follow suit for many
years I was often involved in discussions about
the layout of the new building. Having grown
up looking at architects' plans with my Dad I
enjoyed being part of this project and could
visualise the finished structures and point out
the good and bad points of them. Colour
schemes for curtains and paintwork were also
considered. Although the Unit at the Royal
Surrey has now been open more than twenty

years, only very recently did I manage to visit and see the fruit of these consultations.

Meanwhile, a new fire alarm system that had been installed at St Luke's was proving to be somewhat oversensitive. Arriving on duty one morning I had to get out of the way of a fire engine and followed the firemen into the Labour Ward to find that overdone toast had set off the alarm – we probably incurred a £25 fine for that! Our next false alarm was on a dark weekday evening with the rain lashing down and the site of the problem was indicated as the Pathology Lab. Grabbing an umbrella and a cloak I headed out through the garden and car parks and met the elderly porter who was on duty with the keys. As he opened up we could hear the fire engine approaching! This time water was to blame – coming in through a leaky roof and flooding the alarm box. Another £25 – and then another when, a few weeks later, exactly the same thing happened on the ward ramp outside the Oncology Department.

The next time we really couldn't blame the technology. We clearly saw flames through the window of one of the small cottages just outside the hospital so we called the fire brigade ourselves. Sometime later four burly firemen arrived on the ward laughing and asking for tea. The fire was in the field behind the cottages, which had been gutted ready for demolition, and we had been looking straight through the front and back windows when we saw the blaze! Those days marked the beginning of the end of reliance on telephones with wires and also our iconic red telephone boxes – in 1985 the first British mobile phone call was made and a major change in the way we live was on its way.

One of my regular monthly jobs was the collection of the G85 pay-sheets from the staff in order to collate overtime and weekends worked. Working nights, weekends, evenings and Bank Holidays all attracted a supplement on top of basic pay. I found that it was frequently the same people who had to be chased to complete the forms, but the calculations were not always straightforward – particularly night duty when the clocks changed. In the autumn when an extra hour was worked most people added it on expecting the extra supplement. In spring they were far less ready to subtract an hour and accept the resulting reduction! In actual fact the change to and from British Summer Time made no difference at all to anyone's pay.

During my time as CNS, St Catherine's Ward had to move to a temporary location over the Gynae Ward for three months while work was being done. While we were out, an ex patient volunteered to decorate the nurseries with stencilled circus characters – the end result was beautiful and everyone enjoyed the jugglers and trapeze artists. At the same time we had a washer-drier plumbed in, which made life a lot easier. We lost far fewer mittens, bootees and cardigans when the laundry didn't leave the ward – though it made no difference, of course, to the number of items that left with the patients!

It was decided that management responsibility for Compton Ward, the Children's Ward at Royal Surrey, would come in with SCBU – in other words it would become mine! Since my only experience on a Children's Ward had been six weeks some twenty years ago I was a little concerned about this and tried to visit Compton most days and spent time getting to know the staff. One evening I found them very amused because a child, asked whether he would like fish fingers, baked beans or spaghetti for his tea, had asked instead for "crackers with a little Stilton". They didn't think the NHS could run to that! Paediatric care had moved on considerably since my misadventures with antique electrical appliances at Tite Street, but provision for parents to stay the night was still inadequate and I campaigned on behalf of the staff for facilities to be improved.

Weekends often saw me 'on duty for site' meaning that any of the many and varied problems that could arise in the hospital were mine to deal with. Ensuring every ward was fully staffed for the night should have been a fairly straightforward business – there was a midwifery bank system and another one for the general wards – but to cover each ward in the event of sickness could take many phone calls, and staff often seemed to call in sick at the weekends! Agency help was a last resort as it was very expensive, so my overtime hours – and Lesley's – began to build up.

Once I found myself literally 'helping the police with their enquiries' when, a couple of days after a murder, the local constabulary wanted to question the partner of one of the mums on the ward. He claimed to have visited her on a certain day and I ended up being driven around Guildford and the neighbouring villages in a police car to see if I could point him out to them and confirm his visit. Thankfully I didn't see him!

Another weekend, early on a Sunday morning, a man driving from Woking to Guildford saw a suitcase lying on the grass verge. When he stopped to investigate and opened the case he was horrified to find a baby inside, naked and wrapped in a sheet, not moving and looking, as he put it, 'odd'. He

knew St Luke's because his own children had
been born there, so he quickly closed the case
and phoned the hospital, where he was put
through to me. I at once called the police.

A short while later they arrived on the ward
with the case. It contained a dummy newborn
baby, the sort used by medical students and
anaesthetists to practice infant intubation!
This was quite an expensive – and realistic –
piece of equipment and how it came to be in a
suitcase on the grass verge of the A320
remains a mystery to this day. There were
several theories in circulation at the time but
none were ever confirmed. It was definitely an
experience the man who found it never forgot,
he was really quite shaken.

In the summer of 1985 I had to attend my
fourth refresher course and chose to go to
Leeds so that I could visit Margaret and Ann
who both lived in Yorkshire. The course proved
to be eventful, as one of the younger midwives
who was pregnant developed a deep vein
thrombosis followed by a pulmonary embolism
and needed to be hospitalised immediately.
Fortunately she was not as far from home as I
was and her husband was able to be with her
very quickly.

The following year I took on the leadership of
a home group for Holy Trinity Church. It had
grown out of the original Dales Bible week

contingent and now included the Jones, Peppers, Rawlings and Veness families, with whom we soon forged firm friendships that last to this day, sharing with each other all the ups and downs of life. Holidays and weekends away were arranged to Tonbridge, Bournemouth and the New Forest, as well as involvement with various church activities. During this time I also took on a lot of pastoral visiting for the church, which I found very fulfilling but it did take up a lot of time and energy – both emotional and physical – as did my 'day job'. It was suggested that I might leave St Luke's and work full-time for Holy Trinity as their Pastoral Worker in Knaphill and discussions about this possibility began.

As 1985 passed into 1986 the Unit was increasingly short-staffed and trying to keep it running took up more and more of my time and Lesley's. We often had to put ourselves on call at night and driving into Guilford in the early hours of the morning with the windows down trying to keep awake was neither easy nor safe. I began to realise that, between work and church, I was on something of a treadmill and becoming increasingly exhausted, but I had a holiday in the Isle of Wight booked in August so I looked forward to that and kept going.

The day after I arrived in Seaview I had a massive panic attack. To me it felt like a heart attack and my poor parents were really worried. They called an ambulance, the paramedics were wonderful and an ECG showed nothing wrong with my heart, but that was the beginning of burnout – my body and mind rebelling against the workload I had put on them. I spent the two weeks I had planned on the island and then returned to Surrey, staying with some friends, Stan and Jean Fry. I also started seeing a psychiatrist at Brookwood Hospital and was prescribed medication.

Apart from the clinical depression I had suffered in Harlow I had always seen myself as such a capable person who could cope with all manner of emergencies and it was difficult to accept that I had become so exhausted and unable to do anything. After a time I moved from the Frys to live with Richard and Carol Clark and their sons Graeme and Simon. I tried to help out around the house but had very little energy and was soon tired. They were incredibly kind and patient with me, as I could hardly go out on my own and found driving terrifying. I had also developed a real phobia of large, sharp knives. I am so grateful to all the people who lovingly supported me through this difficult period of my life.

The panic attacks continued for some time, but gradually I learned how to cope with them – though for some time it remained difficult for me to go back to the Isle of Wight where the first one had occurred. While I was ill I received lots of cards from the maternity staff, all saying how much I was missed. When I had been off work for nine weeks the Senior Midwives arranged a supper party for me in one of their homes, which was a great help to me because it meant I could see them all before I returned to the hospital. After eleven weeks I was allowed to work part time and all of my colleagues were wonderfully welcoming. Slowly my energy and confidence began to return and I was less shaky.

I thought this episode would have put paid to the idea of me becoming Knaphill's Pastoral Worker but on the contrary, the church seemed to think that the experience could be a benefit in my understanding of others. For the time being, though, I cut back on church work and resolved to give myself more recreation time and take frequent breaks from St Luke's.

Just as I returned, the long years of campaigning on the subject of caps bore fruit and we no longer had to wear them, so I said goodbye to the frilled pillbox that had sat on the back of my head. I also no longer had the weekly ward-rota 'crossword puzzle' to complete; instead there was a quarterly Unit rota for ward cover by trained staff and Auxiliaries. Since Lesley and I were both examples of the proverb that 'a cluttered desk is a sign of genius' we would borrow the desk of an immaculately tidy colleague on which to spread out the enormous sheet of paper. With no computers to make the job easier it took a lot of time, numerous mugs of coffee and much rubbing out, as we balanced preferences, experience and availability.

The first computer appeared on Compton Ward a few years later, just as I left, but the use of them in hospitals was already gaining ground. Great advances in surgery were also occurring – the first heart lung and liver transplant took place in 1987 at Papworth Hospital, Cambridge, giving the patient an extra decade of life. This would have been unthinkable when I commenced training twenty-seven years before. On the wards we had many more midwives and doctors from overseas as well. I was not present myself but I heard about an occasion in the Delivery Room when an irate father who was already being verbally abusive went to punch an African doctor. This doctor, who had represented his country at boxing, picked the man up under the arms and held him, kicking like a little boy until he calmed down and order was restored.

Now, several decades on, there would be security men to call on, and also a debilitating fear of lawsuits!

The Ockenden Venture (now Ockenden International) was a local charity that looked after refugees from many countries. One Saturday when I was 'on duty for site' I took a phone call from a lady who spoke very little English but I managed to understand that one of the Ockenden residents had recently died in the Henriques (oncology) Ward and that she and another friend wished to come and dress the deceased in national costume. I knew that this would be far from easy but made the necessary arrangements for them to come at two o'clock that afternoon. Before they arrived the porters unlocked the morgue and retrieved the body and I went round removing all Christian articles.

The two ladies arrived, we lit their incense and candles and they brought out the national costume. As I had expected rigor mortis had well and truly set in and I prayed silently that the task would be completed without their friend rolling off the table – since I have never been insubstantial in figure, I was reasonably sure that my side was safe! Always interested in the cultures of other countries I was happy to stay while they offered the prayers of their own religion. When I eventually got back to the

Maternity Ward, everyone I passed sniffed and asked what on earth I'd been doing, as I'd brought the smell of the incense back on my clothing.

The road where I lived in Bisley was always difficult in winter, and when it snowed I often had problems because the big army lorries from Pirbright Camp made massive ruts with their wide tyres, far too big for my little Fiat to fit in. It was also very prone to black ice. I remember early one Sunday morning receiving a phone call at work from my next-door neighbour telling me that a car had skidded, crashed through my fence taking out a number of large rose bushes, and ended up on my lawn facing in the opposite direction to which it had been travelling.

That was the first time I ever claimed on my house insurance. The only other time in the twenty-eight years I lived in Bisley was after the night of October 15th 1987 when the great storm hit the south of England. I slept through it and woke the next morning to find I had no electricity and the corner of my roof had been lifted by the wind. The power was off for five days and I was once more taken in by the Clarkes who only lived a mile away but still had electricity.

There was no chance of an insurance pay-out when my purse went missing because it happened at work and was partly due to my own carelessness. I was in the midwifery offices one evening working on rotas when I got called down to the ward and left my bag by my chair. Returning an hour and a half later I found that my purse containing cash, bank and other cards and postage stamps had gone from the bag. Though the purse was quite a large, bulky one it did not have a lot of cash in it, but I had to inform the bank and the AA and get my cards replaced.

Many months later the gents' toilet in the adjoining ambulance bay was not flushing properly and when a porter climbed up and investigated the cistern he found that the problem was my purse! He brought it, sodden and dripping, and presented it to me, minus the cash but still containing the cards and stamps. At least I now knew the gender of the opportunist thief who had obviously visited my office, seen and swiped my purse, and then gone to the nearest private place to examine its contents. Having pocketed the cash he must have thrown the evidence up into the uncovered cistern.

An instance of misplaced money with a happier outcome involved a five-pound note I had been given in change in the canteen and which I folded carefully into a one-inch square and put in my top watch pocket for safekeeping. I then promptly forgot all about it and it went to the laundry at least twice before I remembered and retrieved it, dried, ironed and perfectly usable.

*

Although twins were a fairly common occurrence I only ever met two families expecting triplets and they both came together, with due-dates inside the same fortnight. The mother of the first set was a blind woman who I had met a couple of years before when her first baby was born. I had heard that she had been admitted to the Antenatal Ward for rest so I went to visit her. I had just begun to introduce myself, "Hello, I'm Sister Roberts and I've just popped in..." when she said, "I know who you are and it's lovely to see you." She had recognised my voice after two years, and still said *'how lovely to see you'* when she couldn't see me at all. Multiple preparations had to be made at SCBU, so that enough midwives, Paediatricians, resuscitators and incubators were available for all six babies. Both deliveries went according to plan and the Unit was bulging at the seams for a few weeks!

The SCBU was a popular cause for fundraisers, especially local schools. Once I was invited to the comprehensive school on the Bellfields Estate to talk to them about the work of the Unit and receive a donation on its behalf. I duly attended morning assembly in the school hall, dressed in my uniform and sitting on the platform with the teachers. Two young people came up and presented me with a most impressive cheque and then I stood up facing hundreds of teenagers – quite a daunting prospect! – and explained to them how their money would be used, giving two or three case-histories as illustrations. They all listened attentively and gave me a great round of applause when I had finished.

Another project I got involved with as CNS was the setting up of a Memories Room with a book for families to record tributes to babies that had died – including miscarriages that had occurred on the Gynae Ward. I used the old general-side CNS office, which was now vacant, and made it as comfortable and welcoming as possible. Rather than the customary 'Book of Remembrance' with names recorded in copperplate, we decided to maintain an informal approach so that siblings could make pictures to stick in or write their own messages. There were no shared pages and no limit to the number of pages each family could use.

Families would often come in on a weekday
afternoon to complete their pages. I would be
there to make refreshments and talk for a
while and then leave them for a time on their
own. Some returned often just to share their
memories and others came to mark
anniversaries. Grandparents would sometimes
come on their own and sometimes together
with the rest of the family. The pages in the
book were really touching to read and the
informality made it so much more intimate
and meaningful.

One very memorable weekend when I was on
duty for site I got involved in a different end-
of-life occasion when a wedding took place in
the Hospital Chapel. The Chapel was
dedicated to St Luke, the patron saint of
doctors (St Catherine was the patron saint of
young women) and was not licensed for
weddings but special permission had been
sought from the Bishop of Guildford and the
Registrar, as this was an extraordinary
wedding – a very sick young lady from
Henriques Ward wanted to be married before
she died. The Chapel was decorated with white
blossoms picked from the grounds – in faith,
because the special permission did not arrive
until lunchtime. The whole service was
amazing and the bride looked beautiful though
she was obviously very ill. Barbara, the Sister

on St Catherine's Ward, reprised the very moving modern duet which she had sung with her own new husband, David, when they got married. The ward staff had transformed a room into a special wedding-night chamber for the couple to share. Unfortunately the bride died the following day, but they had achieved their dream to be married.

By 1988 the NHS was in disarray and nurses were holding strikes hoping to gain pay rises and influence the government to provide more cash for the health service in general. The first strike happened in early February and I well remember driving to work and finding a picket line outside the Antenatal Clinic, though the porters just waved me on and I did a normal day's work. The second strike, two weeks later, happened when I was off-duty. I had already given notice and was due to leave at the end of March and take up my new career as Holy Trinity's Pastoral Visitor for Knaphill on April Fool's Day – I wasn't at all sure what to make of that!

I had three big leaving parties – a lunch party in the Board Room with Senior Midwives, a tea party in the same place for staff of other disciplines, and an afternoon tea party in St Catherine's Ward Nursery – plus a number of smaller tea parties on individual wards. A great number of off-duty staff came in to wish me well, and I was presented with some wonderful gifts including a photo album containing pictures of most of the Maternity Unit staff, which is still a much-treasured possession. There was also an enormous card with added pages, signed by so many people from different disciplines and bearing many messages such as, *"Who will remind me to do my G85 when you leave?"*; *"Thank you for putting up with all my off-duty requests"*; *"You will always be Sister Roberts to me"*: and from Mr Driscoll, *"Invitation. Date: December 25th. Time: 12 noon. Place: St Catherine's Ward. RSVP!"* I was very touched by all of this. It was so nice of the younger staff to make the effort to come in their free time and bring their own babies and children – of course many of those little ones will have families of their own now!

With my car packed full of gifts and flowers I drove away from St Luke's and the medical profession for the last time, twenty-nine years since I had first entered the Royal Masonic Hospital in Hammersmith as a trainee. After all the excitement I was headed for a convivial dinner with my friends the Clarke family, followed by a quiet evening watching *Crocodile Dundee*.

My leaving party in St Catherine's Ward
Nursery

Set 1 1960
L-R back row: Dee Roberts, Maggie Webb,
Margaret MacMorland, Helen Ross, Dee Ward;
front row: Jill Goldup, Evie Vinter

Set 1 1960 Reunion in 2000
Standing: Sue Dadswell, Sue Eardley-Stiff
Seated: Maggie Webb, Paula Lardaux, Ebby,
Mary Coxeter, Helen Ross,

Epilogue

As I write this, quarter of a century has passed since I left St Luke's. The next thirteen years I spent working for Holy Trinity, building bridges into the community. I also tackled some of the administration and organised different events, such as the biennial church weekends at the Salvation Army Training HQ, Sunbury Court, which involved just under a hundred people. I made regular pastoral visits to elderly folk living alone, but also to families where I tried to make myself useful, for instance looking after twins, Abi and Jordan, at teatime so that their mum could spend quality time with their five-year-old sister, Naomi, when she came home from school. I gained some good friends and was invited to school concerts and productions, which I very much enjoyed.

In the first year I introduced a Christingle Service and Advent Candles and my nativity stable, after a few repairs, found a new home in the church with another generation of children having fun arranging the animals. It is sadly no more and I do not have a photo of it but the two decades and more it was part of Christmas celebrations is a testament to the craftsmanship and artistry of the brother and sister all those years ago in Southampton. I enjoyed the challenges that went with my new job but I did miss working in a team and the camaraderie that went with it.

I found that quite a lot of my work was with the elderly, and I set up a group called 'Not So Young' that met monthly for lunch and went on outings to places of interest in the summer and also for Christmas shopping. The summer outings grew into holidays and we enjoyed trips to Worthing, Eastbourne, Torquay, Minehead and Weston-Super-Mare – fifteen in all. A team of volunteers came every year to push the wheelchairs and none of it would have been possible without Eric and Chris Pepper and Christina Hayhoe, but it wasn't all hard work – we had a lot of fun as well. Those who could get into the sea paddled; for those who could not we collected buckets of sea water to pour over their feet as they sat in their wheelchairs. One of my favourite memories is of a wheelchair race one evening along Boscombe Promenade where both passengers were aged around ninety – it was difficult to say which were more competitive, the passengers or the pushers! This, of course would be impossible today, as even the simplest task seems to require filling out a risk assessment form. It probably wasn't sensible then, but it was a lot of fun!

Soon after I began work in Knaphill, an inter-church group was formed bringing

together people from all four local churches –
Holy Trinity, the Baptist and Methodist
Churches and St Hugh of Lincoln Roman
Catholic Church. At this time there was no
real focal point for the village and an idea was
proposed for a café that would provide a place
for anyone to drop into and where everyone,
without exception, would be welcome. It would
be a joint venture between all the churches
and it took several years of planning but, in
1994, The King's House Coffee Shop finally
opened. It was a great success and became a
place of sanctuary for many, as well as taking
up most of my time and energy for the next
nineteen years.

The café was able to provide employment to
young people with special needs from the local
Cranstock Centre and, in later years, we were
privileged to have residents from Alpha
Hospital, a private Psychiatric Unit, both as
customers and volunteers, and to be
encouraged by the progress they made during
their time with us.

In 1997 I took another sabbatical and
returned to Israel, where I spent some time in
Jerusalem visiting projects such as the Helen
Keller Home and School for the Visually
Impaired, and the Princess Basma Centre for
Disabled Children on the Mount of Olives.
After that I went back to Stella Carmel, where I

got involved in the village life of Isfiyah before joining a four-week tour of Israel, researching for the Holy Trinity Pilgrimage that I was planning for 1999. I was now setting my sights further afield than the summer seaside holidays!

The church held a big festival for the millennium and the following February I retired from my Pastoral Worker role and enjoyed another round of parties to mark the occasion. Was I going to be a lady of leisure? Somehow I doubted it! The Coffee Shop was always in need of support and my parents were both in their nineties and becoming increasingly frail (they both died in 2002). A year after that I joined my cousins, Pete, Audrey and Katie, on a holiday to California and had a wonderful time, the highlight of which was a helicopter flight over the Grand Canyon. That was the start of a series of great adventures abroad, including two trips to New Zealand, one to Nepal and four in France, driving round Normandy and the Loire Valley with Christina and Sue. Following my first visit to New Zealand I went to see my cousin, Steve, and his wife, another Sue, in Perth, Western Australia. This was a really enjoyable experience and I found I fitted in well with the Aussie lifestyle.

In 2000, and again in 2010, I took forty-four people to Oberammergau, and in May 2013 I accompanied Holy Trinity's vicar Nick Grew, his wife Christine, and twenty-seven people with varying degrees of mobility to the sites of the seven churches of Revelation where some of us found climbing the steep steps in the archaeological sites to be something of a challenge! On numerous occasions whilst on holiday my nurse's training has come in useful. Once a man in the seat next to me went into a diabetic hypo just as our plane was about to take off, and a girl broke her leg in Crete. During a river cruise on the Danube we took a coach excursion into Hungary and a very large man collapsed a few seats behind me. I went back to see if I could be of help and found him having a massive heart attack; sadly he died leaning on me as I stood in the gangway. At the other end of life's journey, back home in the Holy Trinity evening service, a mum-to-be's waters broke causing a mini flood.

*

As I look back at my years in nursing and midwifery, the words of Gladys M Hardy in her book, *Yes, Matron*, have never seemed so apt: *"Are English nurses happier today than they were twenty years ago?"* she asked (today one might as well say fifty years). *"They certainly have more pocket-money, more freedom, more abundant off-duty time, more social amenities available and their health is constantly guarded, yet I do not believe they are really any happier – if as happy – as we were. So many of them 'live out' and have to make uncomfortable journeys to and from hospitals under the modern conditions of rush and crowded travel. They do not get the feeling of 'belonging' and they lose much by way of friendship and experience. Because the moral tone appears to be not so high and because loyalties are less binding and spiritual values so undermined, they suffer greatly from each other's omissions. Love and sympathy for one another seem to exist in a lesser degree, thus young nurses appear unmindful of the heavier burden falling on their colleagues when they 'steal' extra days off, do not return from holiday on the appointed day, or return to duty very late after a rest period."*

The book was given to me as a school prize in 1954 – six years before I even began training – and was actually written to attract young men and women into the profession! I don't doubt that each successive generation of nurses and midwives would probably say much the same things, though in every generation the majority of them are dedicated to their patients – it is certainly not a job one goes into for the glamour or the remuneration! Nursing, as all professions, is a microcosm of the society in which it operates, and as I touched upon in the introduction, twenty-first century society is changing very fast and not always for the best. Brief return visits to the world of the Maternity Unit, however, have given me cause for encouragement that there are very many 'safe pairs of hands' working there. I still feel that I belong, even after all this time, and a little piece of me always gets reignited when I enter a hospital ward. In 2015 there will be a reunion of 1960's Set 1 from the Royal Masonic Hospital, Hammersmith, where we will gather somewhere in London and catch up on news – all a little greyer, a trifle less svelte and hopefully much wiser!

*

Shortly before this book went to press I was shown around the Maternity Floor of the Royal Surrey Hospital in Guildford – the one I had helped to design. Lynne Argyle, the Maternity Matron was my guide and I remembered her well, as she was in training when I left St

Luke's. She was also one of the nurses on Henriques Ward who helped decorate the Day Room for the honeymoon! I was so excited about my visit and enjoyed meeting the staff in a very different environment to the one on St Catherine's Ward. The only thing that hadn't changed was the warmth of the reception I received.

The King's House Coffee Shop finally closed in July of 2013 and a service of thanksgiving was held that October for all that had been achieved there in nearly two decades. It was in some ways a sad occasion, but *"to all things a season"* – God is always doing something new. What the future holds I have no idea, but I'm sure He has plans for me and I'm looking forward to finding out what they are!